Hunting and Gathering on the Information Savanna

Hunting and Gathering on the Information Savanna

Conversations on Modeling Human Search Abilities

Brian C. O'Connor
Jud H. Copeland

with
Jodi L. Kearns

The Scarecrow Press, Inc.
Lanham, Maryland, and Oxford
2003

SCARECROW PRESS, INC.

Published in the United States of America
by Scarecrow Press, Inc.
A Member of the Rowman & Littlefield Publishing Group
4501 Forbes Boulevard, Suite 200, Lanham, MD 20706
www.scarecrowpress.com

PO Box 317
Oxford
OX2 9RU, UK

British Library Cataloguing in Publication Information Available

Library of Congress Cataloging-in-Publication Data

O'Connor, Brian Clark.
  Hunting and gathering on the information savanna : conversations on
modeling human search abilities / Brian C. O'Connor, Jud H. Copeland ;
with Jodi L. Kearns.
     p. cm.
  Includes bibliographical references and index.
  ISBN 0-8108-4760-4 (alk. paper)
  1. Information science. 2. Information retrieval. 3. Information
storage and retrieval systems—Design. 4. Information organization.
5. Searching behavior. I. Copeland, Jud H., 1943– II. Kearns, Jodi L.
III. Title.
Z665.O28 2003
020—dc21   2003002191

⊖™ The paper used in this publication meets the minimum requirements of
American National Standard for Information Sciences—Permanence of
Paper for Printed Library Materials, ANSI/NISO Z39.48-1992.
Manufactured in the United States of America.

Dedicated with affection to Patrick Wilson

Contents

Figures

Tables

Preface

These pages represent a long-running conversation on human search techniques. The conversation is less a polite fireside chat and more a set of encounters, over pizza and beer, sometimes over coffee, sometimes in one another's classrooms. The snapshots of conversation here range from formal considerations, to speculation, to informal review, to interviews. At times we consider matters in areas with which we have considerable acquaintance; at other times we draw freely from work in fields for which we can claim little authority. It is our hope to provoke deeper and wider ranging exploration of human searching. We hope that those whose work contributes to our pages will find no great fault with our interpretations.

We would, of course, like to thank more than words can say our families and our colleagues at the University of North Texas for their understanding, prodding, and forbearance. Mary Durio did early work with us on "foraging for relevance." Our colleague Richard Anderson helped fashion and critique the foundational model in chapter 1. Thanks to our editor, Sue Easun, who blended praise and pushing in just the right measure. Special thanks to Sally Craley for her patience and deep concern for polishing the details of our work. Gary McAlister and David O'Connor told their stories with care and delight and continued their interest in our conversation. Patrick Wilson sparked interests and planted seeds we hope find expression herein. We would also like to thank our readers in advance for taking the time to engage with these pages, expanding on points they find intriguing, taking us to task for perceived problems, and continuing the conversation.

Brian C. O'Connor and Jud H. Copeland

Chapter 1

Conversations on
Hunting, Gathering, and Information

Brian O'Connor, Jud Copeland, and Jodi Kearns

> ...we spent hundreds of thousands of years as hunter-gatherers without police, without hospitals, and without agriculture. During all that long period of time, slowly, this process of natural selection built or engineered a set of designs which are structured for surviving the challenges of being a hunter-gatherer. (Tooby, in Bingham, 1995)

We might also add that we spent all that time without card catalogs or human computer interfaces. Generation upon generation of our ancestors lived out their lives in a world without books, videos, or the World Wide Web.[1] That we are here speaks to the success of their adaptations. We believe that *hunting and gathering on the information savanna* serves as a focal concept enabling us to stand back from the present, to ask new questions as we grapple with designing more functional and useful means of navigating our information environment.

These pages essentially present a snapshot of ongoing conversations among the authors; they also invite the reader to participate. We use the term *conversation* to reflect our attempts to explore, ramble, and stumble upon ideas with the least prior constraint. We have often sat in each other's offices or at coffee shops discussing the issues found here, though we chose for these pages to present structured units rather than transcripts of our actual chatting. A term used by Van Maanen (1988, p. 7) is appropriate to the design of our work—*intellectual hopscotch*. As in a conversation, we pull pieces from here and there; we speak with different voices; we develop some threads quite fully and leave others to continue to tease us. We hope that these pages will stimulate questions, comments, and criticisms that will advance understanding of human information-seeking behavior. Because the images of human information seeking taking form in these pages are funda-

mentally nondeterministic, we have chosen not to encase them in our
own theoretical constructs. Thus, introductions and conclusions for
each section are kept terse, leaving the reader ample room to construct,
to react, to disagree, and, ultimately, to continue the conversation.

As the manuscript writing drew to a close we continued the conversations on both the topics and the very nature of the relationship
between the reified discussions and readers who come to the work. Jud
came upon another explanatory framework and sent this e-mail to Brian
and Jodi:

> As I review the manuscript for the book, I realize that the
> "conversations" themselves are perspectival tools or accel-
> erators for probing the limits of our understanding about
> experiences in traversing solution space. In this context, the
> book becomes a biography of ideas that attempts to trace
> the emerging outlines of this design process [modeling and
> understanding information-seeking behavior]. We hope to
> capture some of the attributes of the design process in order
> to generate a potential model of problem solving (or the
> experience of traversing solution space) to initiate dialectic
> in the field on this topic. The designation "biography" indi-
> cates the conversations reflect a subjective yet interactive
> process involving different perspectives that are often in the
> shadows. Yet these very perspectives are the attributes that
> will illuminate or define some of the fundamental charac-
> teristics of design that are often overlooked in other re-
> search on this topic. I know this sounds like engineering
> design—I think the whole enterprise really is!

Without specialist knowledge in paleoanthropology or evolutionary psychology or evolutionary epistemology and without linking ourselves to one particular model or school of thought on the exact nature
of our heritage, we presume that we have hunter-gatherer brains and
bodies and some reasonably successful set of adaptations for survival in
a complex and diverse environment.[2] Our conversations assume that
standing back, looking in the shadows, and examining present-day
hunting and gathering activities will provide insights useful to access
system design.

Case stories form a substantial core for the conversations. We
have purposely used the term *stories* rather than *studies* because the
information was gathered ad hoc and, in one instance, quite by happen-
stance. The stories are real-world data evidencing "slippery, abstract
phenomena" (Schamber, 2000, p. 734). Van Maanen speaks to the ability of stories to present "episodic, complex, and ambivalent realities

[and] their radical grasping for the particular, eventful, contextual, and unusual" (1988, p. 118).

The stories here have not been gathered in a uniform manner, subjected to a uniform sort of analysis, or used to identify the same sorts of emergent phenomena. Two were planned as elements of formal research projects; one had been in hand for years—interesting but without appropriate context; one is formed from bits and pieces from several projects that seemed pertinent; and one was simply encountered. One of the stories is based on a grabbed recording made on a moment's notice; two were conducted formally, though originally for a different project; one is based on a formal report of a year-long event; one was cobbled together in a week just to see if anything interesting emerged. We take such diversity as an opportunity for illumination.

It might seem odd that we relate such stories and do so at some considerable length. The stories seem on face value to present quite straightforward question situations. The submarine chaser simply has to find a known submarine; the bounty hunter simply has a name of a person to find; the engineer simply has to find a workable solution to a given problem. These seem to be known-item searches. How might these relate to the scholar attempting to generate new knowledge? Why would we look to stories of contemporary hunting and gathering?

The search for the submarine or the bond skipper is not a known-item search. Rather such a search is for that location and that time when the searcher could intercept the target. In a real sense, the target is almost an ancillary part of the search. The searcher, rather like the scholar, must ask: What is known so that I could be in the right place at the right time? The scholar is looking for a catalyst for new knowledge: What do I know about myself (with regard to this area of investigation) and about the domain of investigation that will bring me to a point of discovery—not necessarily a simple package of preexisting information.

The examination of engineering design, too, is a story, told in the third person about a group rather than an individual, but a story nonetheless. In one sense, the engineering story is a formal presentation of the nondeterministic manner in which humans often solve problems. The logic and notions of classification descended from Aristotle, which have long held primacy as modes of thinking, simply are not the only successful modes. Engineers are demonstrably effective and fundamentally (though, on the face of it, oddly) nondeterministic. The submarine chaser story and the bounty hunter story provide examples of nontrivial searching outside the ostensible realm of engineering. All three stories are told at great length and in considerable detail simply because they represent situations that are complex, messy, nondeterministic, and real. The heart of each lies in the very detail. We take Macbeth's (1996) approach of careful observation of the ordinary in its full detail, eschewing the call to generality, hoping "to come to know them differently" (p. 281).

Setting for the Conversations

Information science has been barking up the wrong metaphor. This assertion emerged over coffee, as we were trying to account for the large number of information searches that fail, even in the digital era. We offer herein a different metaphor informed and enriched by examination of human search capabilities. The epistemological foundation lies in engineering design; the inspiration and elaboration lie in the examination of human search capabilities.

Conversation Participants

As is customary, there is an "About the Authors" statement elsewhere in the book. Since this work is a representation of a conversation, it is of some importance to elaborate briefly on the participants at this point in the text. Brian O'Connor received his Ph.D. from Berkeley in 1984 and is currently coordinator of the Interdisciplinary Information Science Doctoral Program at the University of North Texas. His research interests include idiosyncratic search behavior (e.g., browsing) and representation and retrieval of moving image documents. Jud Copeland received his Ph.D. in library and information management in 1997 from Emporia State University, where he served as dean of the academic library system. In his current position as library director, LeDoux Library, Louisiana State University at Eunice, he continues his work on the philosophical foundations of information studies, as well as management theory. Contributor Jodi Kearns received her Ph.D. from the Interdisciplinary Information Science Doctoral Program at the University of North Texas in 2001. Her research interests center on children's search behavior and children's use of images.

Background

The words here represent conversations we have had over several years. The conversations have often included other colleagues, and we are happy to have a contribution from one of them—Jodi Kearns. This project began when two of us, Jud and Brian, spent hours walking around in a ranch supply store thinking about information retrieval and watching farmers and ranchers find the materials they needed for their livelihood: medicine for cattle, hunting equipment, cotter pins for tractor implements, and lots of things we didn't even understand. There were many signs to point the way to various areas: Paint, Electrical, Ropes, and Machinery. There were also many store workers available to answer questions, point the way to "our implement guy," and to work out possible solutions. There was also a good deal of interchange between customers who evidently knew one another; some of this was social chat and some dealt with business issues: what seed was being used this year, coping with the late rains, and "I hear the catfish are running good over to Chase County."[3] There were numerous sources of assistance in seeking. There was more, as well.

Articulating that "more" provided insights for document searching. We began informally to articulate the different sorts of needs, questions, resources, and encounters we had observed at the ranch store. All of these contributed directly to the livelihood and well-being of the farmers, ranchers, hunters, and their support groups and services. These were added to the mix of our conversations.

Over time and over coffee we considered:

- Wilson's assertion that physical availability does not necessarily mean having access to a document—one must still find some document, then be able to engage it, interpret it, and critique it.[4]
- Borgman's (1996) assertion that online catalogs often fail users because the systems do not account for the vague and iterative nature of many searches.
- The notion of Robertson, Maron, and Cooper of relevance as a relationship between a user and a document under particular circumstances.[5]

Over time we also considered the typical scene for a person whose personal information sources were not adequate for some task. Such a

person would often turn to a library or some database. Only half jok-
ingly, we characterized libraries and databases in the following manner:

- A person visits the library because he or she doesn't know
  something.
- For the majority of people the library is something of a last re-
  sort—after a neighbor, relative, colleague, or personal collection has failed to provide the required information.
- The library says (in the form of its access tools): Tell us what
  you don't know—and do it in system terms.

We thought also about access schemes and how they have generally rest firmly on Aristotelian, deductive logical foundations. In recent
years, the broader range of human thinking modalities has become legitimate. We saw a discipline devoted largely to assisting human information seeking, yet ignoring a significant portion of human classification ability, human search capability, and human search frailty. We
conjectured that if the ranch store operated in the highly constrained
manner of typical document retrieval systems, it would likely go out of
business.

Influences

About the same time, we had the pleasure of a telephone conference
with Fred Hapgood, who had recently written *Up the Infinite Corridor*.
Hapgood had used the story of the Massachusetts Institute of Technology and the individual stories of faculty and student projects to illuminate the "technological imagination." Hapgood's explication of "solution space" presented a rich image, more in keeping with the variety of
search habits, techniques, and necessities we pondered. Concepts reso-
nating with the difficulties of information searching and the methods
used by successful searches included:

- facing the void
- stuckness
- reverence for the fitness of things
- generate, test, examine (embrace) failures, retest.

Hapgood's writing, telephone conferences, and gracious e-mail
contacts gave substantial impetus and support to a doctoral seminar on

information engineering conducted in the School of Library and Information Management at Emporia State University. Epistemological foundations and assumptions were examined closely. Doctoral research growing, in part, from that course resulted in Jud Copeland's dissertation *Engineering Design as a Foundational Metaphor for Information Science: A Resistive Postmodern Alternative to the "Scientific Model."* The substance of this dissertation, and its primary models, form a significant portion of our conversation here.

We continued to be interested in the human aspects of searching. We noticed and we sought out instances of searching and related events. A bounty hunter provided us with a case report for a long and convoluted search. Collegial reaction to an article on scholarly browsing prompted further consideration of scholars in the stacks and online. A grant provided the opportunity to study information-seeking habits of poor inner-city people. Baker's (1994) paean to the card catalog appeared in *The New Yorker*, stimulating conversations on "just why would people be so fond of a tool that is demonstrably ill-suited to its task?" Conversations with Cliff Stoll during his writing of the second edition of *Silicon Snake Oil* generated the thought that humans are spatial and tactile; the tactile delight of dealing with card drawers and the knowing I'm here and the Bs and Cs are over there might just be a better fit with human nature. A subsequent conversation with Don Johanson, discoverer of the early hominid Lucy, followed a similar train of thought.

These pages represent our synthesis of thoughts, conversations, encounters, and research. We present our thoughts, models, and suggestions in the hopes of stimulating more conversation, generating better questions. While this work is not a transcript of a conversation, we have held a conversational tone by presenting pieces in different voices and at varying levels of engagement. Each chapter holds the ideas of all the members of the colloquy, though each chapter has a primary voice noted below the chapter title. We hold no illusions that these concepts are complete unto themselves; we invite critique and engagement in the ongoing conversation.

Information searches fail frequently, in large part, because of

- subject indeterminacy: essentially a significant mismatch between a user's needs and abilities and a system's conceptual tagging of a document and its assumptions about the user (Blair, 1990);
- interface design that ignores more than a decade of user studies (Borgman, 1996).

We can summarize the problematic assumptions of the field as experienced by the individual user with Borgman's outline of why online catalogs are still hard to use:

- User can articulate information need.
- Searches are single (distinct) events.
- There exists a prepackaged answer to the question.
- Searches are topical (when many are functional).

A Foundational Model

For the sake of discussion we posit a simple model of information seeking in human lives. We can say that as each of us progresses through life we encounter varying circumstances, opportunities, and challenges. Each of these requires some form of information input. Much of the required information handling is hardwired or trained into each of us. Our ability to see stereoscopically, our capacities for social interaction, how quickly we can run after a ball or a child about to run into the street, among myriad other tools for processing the raw data we encounter moment to moment, are the result of evolution and early education. Our ability to speak as we do, to read, to stop for STOP signs, to make peanut butter and jelly sandwiches, to determine when it is safe to make a right turn on a red light, again among myriad other abilities are learned well enough so that they can be conducted virtually without conscious effort. Little bumps along the paths of the journeys of our lives are handled by the evolved and learned capabilities.

With some frequency events take place for which the evolved and learned abilities are not sufficient, or, at least, not immediately obviously so. Some of these are of the sort that simply require thinking back to a learned but not frequently used ability or to a known source of help that is not immediately at hand. One might be driving an RV with a 1985 V8 engine from New Mexico into Texas; all of a sudden the engine begins to hesitate and almost stall. Okay—it takes three things to make an engine go: air, gas, spark. What could be going on with one of these three that would account for this condition (that began in a fifty mile-per-hour construction zone with no room to pull out of the way of following traffic)? Unless one is trained in engines to a degree greater than the average driver education course provides, one would need to consult the RV maintenance manual, owner's manual, parts manuals for the fuel pump, carburetor, and so on. One might even feel sufficiently frightened and incapable as to consider calling a tow service and have a mechanic look at the problem. In this instance, a document contains the warning that significant changes in elevation can require that the engine be given different octane fuel—change to a higher octane fuel and the problem evaporates.

What if one is faced with the decision of whether to move far from family and home to take a job that has the potential to be a very positive life step; what if one is in the woods with an ax, a knife, and a canoe without a paddle; what if the baby continues crying and there is no evident reason; what if one sees a funnel cloud drop from the sky in northern California, right onto the road just ahead; what if there is an earthquake and water supplies are cut; what if one is faced with fighting in a war that some judge foolish or immoral; what if one is faced with leaving one's homeland forever; what if...?

We might look at a spectrum of possibilities and responses in the following way. We could say that each person comprises a set of attributes—evolved and learned—and that this palette of attributes may change from time period A to time period B. Some attributes will change little and only slowly—muscular ability, size, understanding of calculus or a foreign language; some may change quite quickly—calculating ability (buy a calculator), vision (new glasses), throwing a ball (Roger Clemens points out that you are releasing the ball a fraction of a second early).

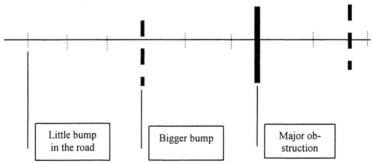

| Little bump in the road | Bigger bump | Major obstruction |

Let us also say that we might represent a person with a snapshot of their current Knowledge State (KS_c). We might think of this as an array of attributes in which some of the cells that would be significant for resolving a situation are empty or have values of no significant utility. Some of these cells have values resulting from evolution, some from education (formal and informal). We can also posit that other people would

A
B
C

E

G

have similar arrays but perhaps have some different cells filled. We can also posit that documents are snapshots of the knowledge states of their authors. So, we might think of a set of documents as KS_{D1}, KS_{D2}, KS_{D3}, KS_{Dn}. Such a conceptualization means that we can treat the individual faced with an information need, other people who may have expertise or advice, and documents as the same sort of entity. Of course, this model would have finer granularity if it were more than two-dimensional and showed the changing values within the cells of the snapshot array over time—accounting for things learned at each little bump, bigger bump, and major obstruction, as well as those things learned by contemplation, chance, and experimentation.

With this model we can then think of information-seeking behavior beyond the realm of recorded documents (the state for a large portion of hominid history and a frequent state even in current times). We can say that confronting an obstruction triggers a recognition of a necessity for a change of state from the current Knowledge State array to a state with cell values adequate to the task—an asking of the question: "What could I or some external source know about the attributes of my knowledge state and the attributes of the problem that would enable the discovery or construction of some category containing both my current state and some pertinent documents (other snapshots of knowledge states), so that I might be able to move to $KS_{adequate}$?" This does not necessarily imply one specific package of knowledge (book or expert), indeed, it might be that considerable resources of time and effort would be required.

There are several consequences of such a model, and there are several layers that have not been explored. For the purposes of our conversations about seeking behavior, this level of presentation helps to frame our case stories as lying outside document retrieval but within information seeking; to recast information seeking beyond the merely topical and into the functional realm; yet to unify all these elements.

Map of the Conversation

We assert that the Aristotelian nature of the field and, thus, its access systems fail to address the whole human engagement with the lived world and the spectrum of questions and seeking patterns that constitute the means of navigating within that world. In chapter 2, "Seeking a Human Orientation toward Problem Solving," we present Copeland's work on discovering a more appropriate metaphor for the field of Information Science and a more useful model on which to ground solutions to the information explosion. The bricoleur[6] model designed by Copeland, and echoing Lévi-Strauss and the pragmatics of Rorty, presents a means for rescuing Information Science by turning the Kuhnian "Are we a science?" dilemma on its head. At the same time, it forms the basis for an expanded concept of retrieval systems, providing the epistemological foundation, the impetus, and a means for exploration of human search capabilities. Here we establish the basis for our conversational approach to illuminating what interesting, vexing, or enabling concepts have been hidden in the shadows.

We look to three different arenas of nontrivial seeking in the next chapters. Chapter 3, "It's Wise to Study the Ways of One's Adversary: Submarine Chasing," explores the thoughts of a highly decorated Cold War submarine hunter. Training, the role of stories, and "knowing the ways of one's adversary" are merged with operations research concepts from Morse and search theory concepts from Janes on browsing and hunting. Chapter 4, "Fifty-Two Stories to an Arrest: Bounty Hunting," examines in depth one case report. Content analysis and discussion with the bounty hunter lead to a multithreaded and dynamic model of seeking, with frequent collaboration and reconfiguring. Chapter 5, "Frameworks for an Emerging Image of Engineering Design," presents a content analysis of the few works on epistemological foundations of engineering design activity. Tolerant of ambiguity, uncertainty, conceptualizing, pragmatic, and visual are some of the concepts that emerge from the examination of engineering design as a human activity.

We move to what has been said in the literature of the field on information hunting in chapter 6, "Foraging for Relevance." The working title for this chapter sets the stage: "Indexing, Coupling, Hunting, and Berry Picking." It should be no surprise that there is not a great deal of literature expressly looking at hunting and gathering behavior. Patrick Wilson seems to be at the heart of the work explicitly looking at information seeking in hunter and gatherer terms. In his book *Two Kinds of Power* he presents a general model and a substantial statement of the necessity for a hunting and gathering model: "We cannot eliminate the need for hunting and picking, for we cannot anticipate all the ways in which people will ask for the items we list in bibliographical instruments."

Perhaps the most widely cited work in this area has been Marcia Bates's "berry picking" article,[7] which articulates descriptions of seeking activity and speaks to means of implementation. Howard White, in *For Information Specialists* (Bates, White, and Wilson, 1992), presents taxonomies of search types and a delightful profile of seekers focused on Katharine Hepburn and Spencer Tracy in *Desk Set*. Brian

O'Connor's (1993) work on browsing is summarized to present a hunter-gatherer model of seeking without recourse to bibliographic tools. This work, too, stems from work with Wilson. Anthropologist Pamela Sandstrom has written of Wilson's work as describing an optimal allocation of resources model. Sandstrom (1994, 1999) has drawn parallels between subsistence foraging and scholarly information seekers. Blaise Cronin and Carol Hert (1995) describe a similar association in the context of the World Wide Web. In each of these there is a strong thread of function rather than mere topicality.

Chapter 7, "Prologue to Dialectic," provides the opportunity to synthesize the results of our investigations and to suggest what a functional access model might look like. There is no intention that we propose one model; rather, we suggest several aspects and attributes of hunter-gatherer searching that are frequently not included in retrieval systems and experiments.

While we were bringing this iteration of the conversation to a close, we encountered a quote from Seymour Papert, professor of learning research at the Massachusetts Institute of Technology, that speaks to the threads that emerged: "Knowledge is only part of understanding. Genuine understanding comes from hands-on experience." [endorsement for Lego MindStorms Robotics Invention System 1.5]

Chapter 2

Seeking a Human Orientation toward Problem Solving

Jud Copeland

Several fundamental crises exist in Information Science. These range from concern about lack of a theoretical framework for the field to the urgent need for solutions to the information explosion.[1] Harris (1986) asserts that many of these issues remain unresolved—he attributes this failure to use of inappropriate models for problem solution. In particular, he characterizes the application of a scientific model in Information Science as "nonsense" and as a "ludicrous misapplication" of positivist technique (p. 529). Gutting (1980) further asserts that use of a positivist line of inquiry in Information Science is "misdirected and fruitless" (p. 84). Indeed, Giddens (1976) argues that researchers who persist in searching for a "social-scientific Newton as a sure path to science" in this field "are not only waiting for a train that won't arrive, they're in the wrong station altogether" (p. 13).

Engineering design as a problem-solving framework holds promise of resolving the crises. Engineers themselves are beginning to address the nature of engineering design as a coherent, human orientation toward problem solving. However, engineering is often neglected or misunderstood as an epistemological entity, especially in the literature of Information Science. Layton (1976) and Vincenti (1990) assert that misconceptions about the nature of engineering have led some researchers to view engineering as mere applied science. In a similar vein, Buckland and Liu (1995) have indicated that some areas of Information Science are so strongly dominated by a "scientific model" of research that they are not able to grasp an appropriate perspective of the potential value of engineering as a problem-solving metaphor for the field.[2]

Issues in Information Science: A Dialectic of Defeat

Kuhn (1970) states that theories are at best only approximations of the reality observed in any given study. Theories and the models derived from them "attach to nature only here and there" (p. 21). In the "interstices" between those points of attachment, one may encounter other theories and models that stimulate a direction for inquiry. Yet researchers often fail to recognize the potential value these theories and models have for advancing their respective investigations.

Harris (1986) argues that there is something "dramatically wrong" with the research orientation of Information Science (p. 515). The prevailing ideology favors adoption of a positivist epistemology for research. This type of thinking is a "scientistic delusion" that has produced an "insular trajectory" in research that in turn has led to a "collective act of intellectual impoverishment" in the field (pp. 515-520). O'Keefe (1993) asserts in a similar manner that such positivist efforts "to enforce theoretical coherence on the field can only work to our collective disadvantage" (p. 79).

Similarly, Buckland and Liu (1995) state that analysis of intellectual frameworks in Information Science has long been neglected and that theory in the field cannot be expected to advance unless alternative sets of assumptions are developed and compared. The long domination of "scientific" logical positivism in Information Science is now being questioned, and theoretical and epistemological assumptions are finally receiving critical attention (p. 389).

Harris feels that this "general malaise of research" signals need for a rethinking of the epistemological foundations of research in Information Science (1986, p. 515). He proposes an orientation that is dialectical in nature. An emphasis on the dialectic challenges the "complacently descriptive approach" of positivism; it questions the search for reductionist answers of "relevance" to complex questions. The dialectical mode of analysis explores the contradictions inherent in any given research inquiry, and it stresses change, conflict, and tension as the foundations of reality rather than stability and consensus (1986, p. 525).

To exercise the dialectic approach effectively, scholars must dedicate themselves to arguing well—the "extended argument" (Harris and Hannah, 1993, p. 145). A dialectical line of inquiry supported by the art of extended argument will enable "the analyst to be far more sensitive to social potentialities than the more conventional positivist approaches" that have dominated the field for more than fifty years (Harris, 1986, p. 525). It will inform researchers in their attempt "to restructure the way they define the 'right' questions and the nature of 'correct' answers" (Harris, 1986, p. 259). Similarly, Debons, Horne, and Cronenweth (1988) assert that critical discourse among information professionals "allows for active exchange of ideas while implicitly verifying the logic of these ideas for their defense" (p. 48). In particular, critical discourse can provide a forum for developing "valid and appropriate" models of engineering design activity. Finally, a scholarly commitment to this process will inform the theoretical orientation of Information Science and provide a framework from which potential problem-solving models for the field may emerge (Harris and Hannah, 1993, p. 145).

Blair (1990, 1992) elaborates on the issue of theory in Information Retrieval. He asserts there is "no unifying vision of what it means to work on Information Retrieval theory, or to build effective Information Retrieval systems" (1990, p. vii). Lacking a theoretical framework, Information Retrieval has been unable to develop appropriate engineering design models to solve problems inherent in document representation and retrieval. Blair does not deny the existence of such models in the field; he simply notes that the models that do exist are "not as easily identifiable" or as well understood as the models one finds in more established fields (1990, p. 298). Blair asks pointedly: "Why can't we build document retrieval systems based on a better understood retrieval model?" (1992, p. 12).

Such issues lead Blair to question the fundamental nature of the field from a scientific perspective. He asks: "Is the study of Information Retrieval a science?" That is, "Do researchers in the field conduct their inquiries in a scientific manner, and do they look at problems which are scientific in nature?" (1990, p. 277).[3] Blair responds with a "Kuhnian paradigm analysis" (Gutting, 1980, p. 88) of Information Retrieval. He concludes that the field has many scientific components and that from a "strictly Kuhnian perspective," Information Retrieval must be viewed as a pre-paradigm or revolutionary field. From the standpoint of engineering models, this implies that there are several candidate models emerging in the field and that no one model has yet gained "ascendancy" in the field. Blair even asks: "What might some of these models look like?" (1990, pp. 297, 305).

Entman (1993) states that potential research paradigms in Information Science have "remained fractured with pieces here and there but no comprehensive statement to guide research" (p. 51). He proposes the concept of "framing" as a means of bringing together insights and theories that would otherwise remain scattered in other disciplines. Framing

is a potential technique for enhancing the theoretical rigor of scholarship in research. According to Entman, framing essentially involves
selection and salience. To frame is "to select some aspects of a perceived reality and make them more salient" (meaningful, noticeable) in
a research inquiry ... in such a way as "to promote a particular problem
definition, causal interpretation, and/or solution recommendation" for
the object of study (pp. 51-52).[4] Entman's concept of framing, selection, and salience stimulates theory and model development for engineering design.

   Kahneman and Tversky (1984) posit ideas on framing that relate
to assumptions underlying a theory and model of engineering design
activity. The authors characterize the concept of framing as a "meta-
theoretical stance" or technique that selects and illuminates some fea-
tures of reality while omitting others. In other words, while frames (for
theory and model development) may call attention to particular aspects
of the reality described, they simultaneously—and logically—direct
attention away from other aspects of the phenomenon under investigation.

   Most frames are defined by what they omit as well as include. The
omissions of potential problem definitions, interpretations, and solutions may be as critical as the inclusions in guiding the researcher
(Kahneman and Tversky, 1984, pp. 343-344). In other words, the selection of a particular research frame (design) not only directs but also
limits the types of questions that may be asked during a given inquiry
(O'Keefe, 1993, p. 78). Capra states "the patterns scientists observe in
nature are intimately connected with the patterns of their minds, with
their concepts, thoughts, and values." He further notes that empirical
data from their tests are conditioned by their "frame" of mind. "The
sharp Cartesian division between mind and matter, between the ob-
server and the observed, can no longer be maintained. We can never
speak about nature without, at the same time, speaking about ourselves" (Capra, 1982, pp. 86-87).

   Edelman (1993) addresses this issue in stating:

> The character, causes, and consequences of any phenomena
> become radically different as changes are made in what is
> prominently displayed, what is repressed and especially in
> how observations are classified. The social world is...a ka-
> leidoscope of potential realities, any of which can be read-
> ily evoked by altering the ways in which observations are
> framed and categorized. (p. 232)

This is why exclusion of interpretations by frames is as significant to outcomes as inclusion.

Sniderman, Brody, and Tetlock (1991) state that a potential "counterframing" of the subject is absent in most research inquiries. They assert that counterframes can provide researchers with alternative ways of thinking about their research engagement, and, perhaps more important, they can provide alternative perspectives for viewing problem definition, interpretation, and solution in any given research inquiry (p. 52). Indeed, counterframing can assist researchers in their "initial attempts to elucidate [the] topographical details" of their investigation (Hoyningen-Huene, 1993, p. 175).

Engineering Design Epistemology

Kerlinger (1977), author of "a highly respected text on research methodology" (Rudestam and Newton, 1992, p. 6), asserts that "the basic purpose of scientific research is theory and model development" (p. 8) for confronting the problems of natural phenomena. He cites Nagel's (1979) work as "the most detailed, cogent and comprehensive defense for use of scientific theory and models in the field of research" (Kerlinger, 1977, p. 9). Kerlinger encourages scholars in the social sciences to adopt Nagel's ideas as a fundamental starting point for their research. Nagel's notions about theories and models in science have implications for model development in engineering design.

According to Nagel, scientific theory has a defined tripartite structure that comprises

> an abstract calculus that is the logical skeleton of the explanatory system, and that "implicitly defines" the basic notions of the system; a set of rules that assigns an empirical content to the abstract calculus by relating it to the concrete materials of observation and experiment; and a model for the abstract calculus, which supplies some flesh for the skeletal structure in terms of familiar conceptual or visualizable materials. (1979, p. 83)

In sum, any given scientific theory embodies an abstract calculus (explanatory theory); a set of operational definitions (for assigning empirical content to the abstract calculus); and a model (for interpretation of the abstract calculus). Nagel claims that his "abstract calculus" can be used to "implicitly define" the basic notions of systems in the social sciences and other fields. He further claims that the set of rules derived from empirical observation and experiment can lead to effective "model generation" (p. 85) in these fields. What type of model would Nagel's "abstract calculus" generate for engineering design? Would such a model be appropriate for design activity?

Ferguson (1992) argues that any model of design activity based on Nagel's scientific "formula" is problematic. It implies that design is a formal, sequential process that is deductive in nature. Design is perceived as discrete, linear segments that, if followed according to Nagel's prescribed order, lead to predictable outcomes. Billington (1996) supports Ferguson's argument concerning the assumptions underlying Nagel's scientific formula. He states that

> formulas do not solve problems. Formulas suggest designs, stimulate insights, and define limits, but they never provide ways to the best solutions, as so many technologically illiterate writers on engineering [design] suppose. Formulas do not define a "one best way" or an optimum. Formulas represent a discipline, not a design; they can never ensure [an]...essential elegance. (p. 4)

Dupre (1993) further asserts that theories and models derived from the "prestige of science" reflect a kind of assumed unity that has no genuine consequences for engineering design epistemology. The term *scientific* (as in Nagel's application of the term) has become

> an epistemic honorific quite independent of any general consensus about what makes scientific claims any more deserving of credit than beliefs from any other source. The entitlement to this pseudoepistemic power and the extent of this hegemony are depressingly illustrated and parodied in the absurd or banal claims made by actors in white lab coats in television advertisements. (pp. 221-222)

In reference to "art, imagination, and the scientist," Root-Bernstein (1997) asserts:

> The road to objectivity in science is paved with subjectivity. Einstein, who is often quoted as saying that in creative science, "imagination is more important than knowledge," also noted that despite the objective nature of scientific results, "science in the making, science as an end to be pursued, is as subjective and psychologically conditioned as any other branch of human endeavor."

In Nagel's scientific theory, the object of experiment, proof, and analysis is "to expunge this subjective residue from the final statements of scientific fact." But to ignore the subjective, "even idiosyncratic origins of imaginative ideas in science is to cripple its creative potential" (Root-Bernstein, 1997, p. 6). Shortland (1981) also challenges Nagel's scientific assumptions. He asserts, "[T]he trouble with Nagel is not so much with what he examines as in the serious things he has left unexamined" (p. 475). However, the "greatest danger" lies in Nagel's assumptions about use of scientific theory and models in the social sciences. Shortland cautions scholars in adopting approaches "that imply a strong, positivist orientation in their line of inquiry." He further asserts that "none of the cosmetic readjustments" made in Nagel's revised edition (1979) of his work justifies application of his "abstract calculus" theory to other fields (pp. 476-477, 480).

From within the field of Library and Information Studies, Patrick Wilson (1977) has called for "a reorientation toward the functional rather than topical or disciplinary" in the organization and representation of documents; this shift is "one that explicitly recognizes the primacy of the need to bring knowledge to the point of use" in problem solution in Information Retrieval and Information Science (Wilson, 1977, p. 120). The "growing undercurrent of urgency" (Blair, 1990, p. viii) imposed by the technological explosion echoes Wilson's ideas and provides impetus to look beyond the traditional, positivist approach to problem solution. Wilson further asserts that

> the final test of the adequacy of decisions is in the consequences. If we are happy, or at least satisfied, with the results of our decisions, we have no cause to complain about the antecedents of those decisions, including the information supply on which they were based. If events turn out well, in our eyes, then we have no basis for criticism of our role in bringing about the events or of the information supply we used. (1977, p. 68)

Following the positivist mode of thinking leaves no avenues to address the problems besetting Library and Information Science. Indeed, there is an increasing sense of "incredulity" over the ability of a "legitimized scientific metanarrative" to solve these problems (Lyotard, 1979, pp. xxiv, 27). Wittgenstein's "perspicuous examples" are the critical link to understanding that information seeking is a pragmatic and contingent activity (Blair, 1990, p. 157).

Florman (1994) states that engineers are experiencing a "heightened level of awareness" that there are alternative modes for problem solving based on perspicuous examples of engineering design. Post-modernism gives expression to some of these emerging modes of think-ing. In particular, Foster (1985) illuminates the postmodern context that is appropriate for a model of engineering design as a human problem-solving activity.

The "reactive" postmodern approach to problem solving involves "recycling old and discarded concepts—it deals in claimed certainties, 'the perfection of the past' or the 'past-perfect'—even though the past to which it refers is not the actual past but merely a nostalgic illusion of it." Similarly, Foucault (1972) states that a reactive postmodern ap-proach ignores the knowledge that it is an illusion that the past can ever be known, let alone certain. In contrast, the "resistive" version of post-modernism "deals with the real uncertainties of the world, 'the imper-fect future' or 'future-imperfect.'" Whereas reactive postmodernism can never offer more than more of the same thing recycled, resistive postmodernism does at least offer the possibility of a "radically new understanding" of problem solution in a human context (Jackson and Carter, 1992, p. 16). Resistive postmodernism "inescapably presents itself as a new language" that can de-center the "albatross of scientific rationality" in approaches to problem solution (Foster, 1985, pp. 13-16).

A resistive postmodern perspective involves the "fundamental questioning of a totalizing rationality based on science" (Jackson and Carter, 1992, p. 12). It illuminates potential problem-solving methods that "a dominant modernist style of thinking pushed into the shadows" (Cahoone, 1997).

Our conversation is intended as an opening dialectical response that challenges the "positivist definition of epistemological rectitude" cited in Information Science theory and research (Harris, 1986, p. 526). It is intended to stimulate an "extended argument" for alternative ap-proaches to problem solution in the field. Engineering design can be shown to be a coherent, epistemologically sound, human orientation to problem solving in the field generally termed *Information Science*.

Chapter 3

"It's Wise to Study the Ways of One's Adversary": Submarine Chasing

Brian O'Connor

In October of 1998 I had a significant information encounter.[1] On a train heading out of Chicago and bound for Texas, I responded to the first call for dinner. Upon entering the dining car, I was greeted by a steward who sat me at a table with three other diners—a retired geologist and a couple recently retired from the Navy. During the small talk as we waited for our meals, I mentioned my work on information retrieval and, because of the Navy folks, I brought up the work of Philip Morse bringing wartime submarine and air search concepts into the realm of document searching. The man from the Navy excitedly shared that he had spent many years as a submarine chaser. This was the start of a three-hour conversation about how one finds submarines in the open water.

Gary McAlister later met with me for a taped interview about submarine hunting. He also provided videotapes of his retirement ceremony that, among other things, provided evidence of his accomplishments—he is recognized as one of the best in the Navy keeping track of Soviet submarines during the Cold War era. He also recommended other sources of information, not the least of which was the film version of *The Hunt for Red October*.[2] He notes that the character Jonesy, while in the submarine rather than the search plane, displays all the best characteristics of a hunter: thorough knowledge of the environment and machinery, deep familiarity with how boats and their commanders operate, and an almost obsessive attention to details, especially those that are out of place.

The interview took place outdoors under a park shelter in Gainesville, Texas, between thunder showers. The transcript has occasional gaps where sensitive material has been deleted or abridged or where obviously irrelevant material—such as our discussion of the cream pie we had eaten before the recording session—has been deleted.

Transcript of Discussion with Gary McAlister

GM: When I started out I was an antisubmarine warfare operator.[3] They changed it right at the end of my career, to where I was an antisubmarine warfare systems operator, meaning I could do anything. That wasn't the truth.

One of the questions you asked was looking for the characteristics that would bring you to the submarine like Wayne Gretzky came to the puck. I know you said that, and that's been quoted, but I don't feel in my particular case that that was the same. I felt like very early on in my career that I was given the [gosh I hate to use the word *gift*—I hate that concept, I'm going to call it] *luck*. On my very, very first mission, I made a call that was overruled at the time and then reinstated later after [mission] analysis, looking at the anatomy of the whole mission. And that kinda just catapulted me into some kind of legacy.

Figure 3.1. P3C Orion. U.S. Navy Photograph

I hated that, because where do you go from there? I'm brand new at the job. Everybody's looking at me. And there were people that were vying for my attention to be moved to a different crew, saying, "If this kid is that good I want him over here." Even the commanding officer of the squadron at that time said, "I want that kid on my crew." That diminished quickly, although I was successful at finding and maintaining contact on top of submarines. My favor with the squadron left pretty quick. I had a young lieutenant call me "a son of a bitch" and I told him straightly: "I don't appreciate you speaking of my mother that way and you can kiss my ass." Well I lost a rank or ended up not being promoted. Several other heads fell along the way as it turned out.

But my prowess or luck, or whatever you want to call it, continued. They threw me away, the squadron basically threw me away, because of that incident with the lieutenant. And they sent me someplace where I had to do lots and lots of research, tons of research, writing a new training program to teach other people how to do what I had basically stumbled upon.

BOC: So when you were doing the research, were you talking with other people?

GM: It was all team. ISDT is what it was called—Instructional Syllabus Development Team—with civilians as well as scientists. They based all of their instruction on real-world people who had experienced it. It was involved with Lockheed as well as Magnavox and lots of other people. We were the foundation of this thing—writing problem situations, looking at oceanography, the topography of the bottom of the ocean—but that's what it was about. We studied that hard and we called people in and asked: "Have you ever been in this part of the ocean? And experienced a submarine encounter?"

I did that for about nine months, and I made rank while I was there and left there highly recommended for anything in the world. Well there goes the myth again. My initial encounter was now promulgated again to another level, and I hated it some more. But because of that I was allowed to go to this tiny, small, third-world country called Bermuda. And I had to suffer [said with a wink and a smile] there for three-and-a-half years. But while there I met two people. One was a master chief—old, old guy who started out his submarine hunting in balloons and helium crafts—by the name of Ken Ickies. We called him The Boss just because he had done it so long. And the other one was a guy by the name of Tommy E. Davis, and he was just getting ready to retire. I learned more from watching him, just looking at what he did.

There was so much that had to go on. I had to do hours of training. There was aircrew coming and going [that] had to be briefed and debriefed, and replays that had to be done and computer things. And out of all of that I learned some, but watching Tommy Davis was the most giving and just—let me think if I can capture a word—*he just knew.* He was before technology. He was before computers. He had so many stories, and I would sit and listen to him when we were at the beach or the ballpark. He'd say: "Gary Mac, you know this and that and you gotta do this. Think this way. If it's this boat then it's probably this skipper. If it's this other boat it's probably this skipper." He didn't retire in Bermuda. He retired out of Florida.

But while I was still in Bermuda, we got in a situation where we didn't know what the then Soviet Union had planned. The ocean is divided into sectors as far as antisubmarine warfare is concerned. It's like deer leases. You can hunt over here and you can hunt over here and you can hunt over here. For years, the Soviets had been in a routine where they had done everything pretty precise; we knew which boat was coming when, we knew which skipper was going to be where, at what time; and that's how we trapped it. Back in the late 70s or the early 80s, something happened that we did not know. We, and I'm talking I was the bottom of the food chain, all of the big guys did not know that airplanes started landing in Bermuda and started off-loading so-called experts. They were the ones who where going to look at this stuff and figure out why the Soviets ... were doing what they were doing. And basically what happened was that there was just a multiple of ballistic and intercontinental-type submarines in the Bermuda sector all at the same time. And we didn't have enough airplanes to find them. We couldn't track them, and refuel and get them back out with enough people all at the same time. So we got on the phone and called the Canadians. They sent a couple airplanes down. Called Jacksonville, Florida, they sent several airplanes. But the tracking concept still didn't work. Something Tommy shared with me is if you don't think like those people think, then you're not going to be able to catch them.

BOC: Like a good cop has to think like a criminal.

GM: Pretty much. But what he did say was: "What's happening here, Mac?" Now you gotta think of the financial situation of the United States in 1980-81. The financial situation of the Soviet Union was disastrous. But all of their money was banked on this nuclear capability they had. By putting all those submarines in that small box—small, relatively small, thousands of square miles of ocean, but relatively small—the mid Atlantic runs through there and the trench on both sides, that's a lot with the Gulf Stream flowing through there. Lots of stuff going on. They were able to power check our capabilities to monitor what we were doing and what we were capable of.

The mission, though, was to have an airplane with a deliverable weapon on top all the time. We couldn't do that so we had to set up new tactics. In other words, to find them. I told you about the old man, The Boss, Ken Ickies, he came to me in the middle of the night and said: "Mac, I've never dealt with anything like this before. And we've lost one, we've got four, one is missing. What would you suggest?" I'm a kid at this business! I'm just a babe in the woods and here's the oldest guy in the world, he's been doing it forty years, asking me, and I said: "I don't know. Why would you trust me? There are other guys." And he goes, "I've made a phone call. They say you're the best." I hated that. I mean I loved Ken Ickies. I loved him well. I loved his family. But I hated that pressure. What if I'm wrong?

BOC: That was one of these things on that [television documentary on training submarine officers] show last night, when they were talking about training those new officers. The hardest thing being: What if I make a mistake?

GM: I drew on what limited experience I had, what specified experience by having to go to the books, by having to dig deep, by having to understand the oceanography, the topography of the bottom of the ocean. But by doing that I was able to draw on that limited knowledge and experience I had, and by watching Tommy Davis do it, by watching him, the best of the best—and this guy used to joke; I'd say: "What are you going to do when you retire?" He'd say: "I'm gonna go down to Louisiana and I'm going to open 'Tommy E. Davis Submarine Finding Company.'" He says: "I'll be the damnedest doggone finest submarine finder you can ever get." I don't know what he's doing today; I lost track of him. But when this came about I called him. I called him in Virginia. He went to Fosic, which I believe was the enemy with all the hubbubs and mucky-mucks. On the East Coast, they think they know what they're doing but they're not out there. And we solved the situation. Found that one. Got on the phone, called in support from other squadrons and countries; the French came in, the British came in. And we were at a scary situation having five nuclear submarines with missiles aimed at the United States in the west Atlantic area. And you may remember the one that got trapped in the fishing net, that came up. That was all part of that situation. That was once or twice. I guess my point is that I was fortunate—lucky at first, fortunate after, and relied upon thirdly.

BOC: The idea that you were able both to observe and hear the stories of real experts and see the value in them [seems to have been very valuable to you].

GM: Well, the people that did it well never [bragged] on the next one. That was something laid on them by somebody else. And you can go through my cruise books. I was looking at them, and I'm going, "Wait a second. Wait—if I was that good, where's all the pictures?" And the only pictures there are with my crew, and [there are] guys in normal uniforms, the officers, the flight suits are nice and pressed. And I'm kneeling down on the ground sweating my balls off just trying to be there for the picture, get it over with, and I'm out of here. I got some thing to do.

BOC: I've got a sub to find.

GM: Well, or something else. It wasn't just, get on an airplane, go find a sub, and come back. That was one of your questions: "What kind of preparations does this take?" It's [humongous]! It's huge. It's an enormous team effort. But once you're there, it's just almost one on one. I don't care if the information I ask you doesn't work. If you can't sort it out and actually locate and get a weapon on top of this guy, I don't care. I cut it off at my wall—where my station was, and the kid who sat next to me was, which they're identical—but it was my job to make sure he was doing the right thing and that I was directing him. That was the kind of pilot–copilot thing I suppose, except it goes the other way. I wanted it for the success of the crew but it was more important that I did everything that I could to make that capture: "I got him by the tail, now you rope him, or do whatever it is you want to do with him."

It happened again in the year they didn't make a cruise book. We had a fragmented crew, meaning everybody who needed to be with us was in, some were sick, whatever. And they gave me a young airman; they said: "We've lost a submarine." The goal or the mission was to keep in touch with all of the missile submarines all over the world—a huge, huge concept, but important, thinking that each submarine may have eight, ten, twelve, twenty missiles on it, and every missile with six, eight, ten warheads on it. That's a scary concept. One of those things lost [is a major problem] … [since just] one [carries a whole country's worth] of munitions. If you think that way [it's frightening] … but they lost one!

BOC: When you went out did you go out for two days, six hours, or…?

GM: Six months. When I left home I was gone six months. Each mission was about anywhere from an hour to two hours in briefing; three hours of preflight, just getting the airplane ready to go, making sure the equipment was optimal. And then ten to twelve hours of flight. My longest flight was fourteen hours, ten minutes. That's 'cause we took off out of Okinawa and the submarine was <finger snap evident on audiotape> right there. We knew gas was just barely over the horizon. So it ended up, after postflight and debriefing, about a twenty-three-hour day. And then fifteen hours, not from the time you finish debriefing, but from the time the wheels touch the ground, fifteen hours later, you started it again.

BOC: So was there then a second plane that took your place? Did you have blanket coverage?

GM: Usually, we'd put a sensor in the ocean. He's here. We have contact on this sensor. We're departing to the west. You come from the east. Mark that sensor. And they'll say, "Yes we have contact." And start out. And then we'd go home and get gas and something to eat. Rarely I called there … the first thing you did when you got home was read the flight schedule. Party! Someone's got it iced down. In the old days we used to keep a cool of beer on the airplane. Just go, yeah! We're not on flight schedule; let's hit it. We'd get on the ground and start drinking beer.

BOC: Maybe I won't put that part in the book.

GM: It's been in books before. That other situation—what I was going to tell you. … We were in Okinawa and a [Soviet] submarine was doing odd things, an older submarine. Old, easy to track, lots of noise. It didn't matter, but what was he doing? We followed him through the Sea of Japan and the Tsushima Strait, and down around the South China Sea, and there had been several crews involved with it, but I had the opportunity to be on it several times. And then they did the oddest thing: they just headed for Hawaii. We were expecting him to head off to the Indian Ocean somewhere; he turned left, and we're going, "Hello? This is a little bit different." He hit the Marianas Trench off of the Philippines. He went deep, stayed deep. And I'm just going, "This is weird." … The hackles come up. "This is not right." And I'm trying to tell people, I said: "Watch this sucker, he's not doing the right thing."

I got in trouble again. They said: "You don't know your ass from a hole in the wall." I said: "Look. There's no reason to take an old boat and do this kind of stuff with it. They've done too much." And he did. He did exactly what I said he would. He turned left. He went to the

Marianas. He went through it for a while, took a gap out of there, and headed straight to Hawaii. Now this was an old level-one Soviet nuclear boat. It just kept going, and they launched all kinds of crews and launched us. That was the best crew I ever flew with. Except, I had a new tactical coordinator, he was a commander, an 05, and this kid, Pat Pereni, sat next to me and I said: "It doesn't matter. I can do this by myself." That was basically what I was feeling at the time. I said: "I know what I'm talking about. We gotta go with this." And in the back of my mind, I'm going, "What would Tommy Davis do?"

I met another guy that year—in fact that very year—Donny Ray Perkins, another [who] came out of antiquity and watched technology push him aside. He knew, he knew what was going on.[4] So his crew, and my crew, headed east towards Wake and Midway; we're going home. And Okinawa—we're supposed to be there six months. Here's Hawaii, here's Wake, here's Midway, here's Guam, here's Hawaii, and we're going that direction chasing this one submarine. And we lost him several times because we just couldn't believe that he would keep going that far. We'd gotten set in those boxes. They stay in those boxes.

Uh oh—the anomaly: something's different, something's wrong. I was fortunate to be on top of this guy enough that I knew everything about that boat. Every machine change. I could tell when they were mixing margaritas in the kitchen. I just had looked at it and when I came back, I didn't sleep, I didn't go to the clubs; I just sat down and I looked at the paper and I said, "There's standards here. There's things that do not go away." But he continued. Then they got into a political war. Once he [leaves] the box, whose submarine is it? Is it Seventh Fleet? Is it Third Fleet? So we'd have to turn around and go back over here, and they'd go: "Okay, we got him" and they'd lose him. Then he'd come back to our box and here we'd come again. Put some gas on, get a couple hours of sleep. Over here right up against that line. We'd chase him around; and he'd go over here and we'd have to turn around and go back. And they'd say: "OK, we got him." We flew so long on that single contact, that the admiral came down and said: "I've got to ground you. You've been in the air too many hours. You're not safe anymore." He brought a flight surgeon down to look at us, evaluate us.

I was saying: "Is that crew going to fly out? Put me on that crew. It's a strike of a pen which crew I fly on, I don't care. Let me go. I gotta figure out what that guy's doing." But they grounded us and flew a crew from Japan to come get us. They wouldn't even let us fly back to Japan. With that, while we were sitting on the ramp ready to leave, engines had already started, ready to pull out and go, they come out and shut us down, and called for our mission commander, my crew's mission commander, to step off the airplane. And they're going: "All right you suckers, someone went out on the town and caused some trouble last night. Who's getting arrested here?"

[Instead] they pulled us off that airplane, fueled up another airplane, and put us back in the air because they felt that we were the ones that could recapture that submarine. Now, I talked to you early on about how I hate that pressure. We're out in the middle of the Pacific Ocean.

BOC: Which is a big place.

GM: It's one of the biggest ones around. Somewhere between Hawaii and Guam they've called up the war reserve on sensors. The concept was that it had been passed off to another sensor. I don't know exactly what that means, but I suspect that maybe a fast-attack submarine had been put on its tail to watch this thing, keep it in its sight. He probably is not employed now, the skipper of the submarine that lost him. This old crotchety level-one nuclear Soviet submarine lost by this top-of-the-line world-class nuclear submarine. *Hello! Somebody's in trouble!* And they put us back on an airplane, and within an hour we were fueled and loaded and in the air. And within two hours of taking off I had him again. There's that pressure again.

BOC: So what did you do? How did you figure that out?

GM: I'd watched him for so long—here's that box, here's one fleet's responsibility, here's another fleet's responsibility—and what he had been doing was ham stitching that box. And it was ever so many hours. It's what he had done.

BOC: So it looks like he is purposely jerking your chain.

GM: Billions of dollars expended just to figure out what this guy is doing. We know later why, and if you read the John Walker story—big spy guy; big submarine guy—it's all part of this. That's all he was doing: just jerking our chain. And I said: "You cocksucker, I've got you! I know where you are." And he'd turn around and come back and [do] it again. And again the luck thing came in. And I told my tactical officer: "Look, you go straight to the line and you light a death barrier"—I call them death barriers because you get bored to death waiting for them to come alive—but I said: "You lay a death barrier up there and you put me a direction buoy on each end and I'll find him." But I did something else [too]; I studied the oceanography very, very closely. And they said: "You're not scientific enough." I said: "I know this stuff. I don't have to be scientific." I said: "You put me two buoys in the water, seven miles apart, and I'll read the ocean for you." And they have something they call a figure of merit, where it gives you a 50 percent probability of detection. Now that's not good enough. You gotta do better than that.

BOC: I'd buy a lottery ticket for that, but I'd hate to stake the defense of the country on it.

GM: Fifty percent probability of detection: that's what a figure of merit is. But that deals with the speed of sound in the water, the frequency of sound that you're looking for. Some frequencies are better than others. The higher the temperature, the higher the speed of sound. All kinds of stuff involved. But I'd studied that, where we were going. But it was the line that was the key part, and I could not get this guy to believe it. And finally I talked him into it. He said: "You show me your FOM, your figure of merit, and you tell me what you're thinking and I'll go with it." So I said, "Fine." So we laid this thing out there. It was supposed to be out there for eight hours. And I just laid back and went to sleep. I just kicked my chair back, tucked my hands in my life preserver like this so they don't fall around and hurt anybody. I would sleep. Kept my headphones on of course, because it's a multisensual thing. It's not just sight. It's not just knowledge. It's here. It's feeling; it's lots and lots of stuff.

And this kid all of a sudden next to me goes: "Mac! Mac! Wake up! I think we got him! I think we got him! I think we got him!" And I'm looking and I'm going: "We got him!" And I turned around to my ordinance [guy]—I didn't even ask permission—I turned around to my ordinance [guy] and said: "Put a buoy out now!"

Foom, he went; foom, the buoy is gone. TACCO [Tactical Coordinator] goes: "What the hell was that?" I said: "Oh sorry, Buoy Away!" He goes: "What buoy?" I go: "I already reached over while you were napping and dialed it in." He was so pissed off. This was a full commander. He was an 05; you know, next would-be captain in the Navy.

We had the son of a bitch. He did what I'd counted on. I knew what he was going to do. I knew I could watch him and I told him: "Okay, you wait a second; okay, we got him." He's changing modes. He's flipping switches, turning off turbines, and all kinds of stuff. He's fixing to come up to talk to the Russians and see what they want him to do. They said: "How can you know this?" "I know this skipper, trust me." I said. "The sun is coming up in fifteen minutes. By the time the sun comes up, give me a sea [reading], how tall are the waves out here?" And they were about twelve feet, you know, smooth ocean but twelve foot curling swells of wave. She'll broach, come through the water. He's gonna have to get close enough to the surface to talk to his people and we're gonna catch this guy on the surface. And the sun came up, and one minute after sunrise we were right down his periscope flying straight in to him. Just like that!

And they said: "Mac, how did you know that?" I said: "Because I read the book. I studied this guy. I watched him." We had flown thirty something missions on this guy. Thirty times ten is three hundred hours. "You guys don't look at this stuff. You don't talk to the other operators. You brag about your take-offs and landings. You're pilots not analysts." There's that pressure still building.

BOC: Wayne Gretzky says: "I skate to where the puck is going to be." People think it just comes; yet it only comes because they put everything into knowing how…

GM: I had difficulty understanding that question. I'm not a hockey person. There's a round rink. I went to a street fight one time and a hockey game broke out.

BOC: It's like calling somebody an overnight success, a performer, you're not…

GM: Well, twenty-five years is not quite overnight.

BOC: And I think it's the people like you. You knew this guy in every sense.

GM: I wanted him.

BOC: You hear, you feel, you know what he's going to do, and you know where he's operating.

GM: I didn't want him personally. But it was good enough that the admiral showed up in Guam, when we got back after the recapture, and the turnover to the other sensor. The admiral showed up and he looked at me and he looked at the mission commander and said: "If you guys don't go back to the Philippines first and have T-shirts made, the greatest crew on earth, or something, you don't have a hair on your balls. You better go back to your squadron proud." As it turned out, this was a huge political debate. The federal government, the knot-heads—I won't call them warheads—in Washington wanted to keep this hush-hush because they were embarrassed that their big bucks had not [paid off].

BOC: It must be embarrassing. Those look like propellers there to me on that plane. The idea that—

GM: Pinwheels, I call them. There are only six things on that airplane that will kill you. Those four and these two idiots sitting right there around that guy in the middle.

BOC: The idea that a prop job is out there doing...

GM: Well it's a lumbering dog, literally. It'll do about 430 miles an hour straight ahead. On the job, about 160 miles an hour 200 feet off the water, yanking and banking through fog and snow and ice and clouds. Operators [are] back there puking their guts out. And you can't get out. Never use an airbag twice. Trust me. Use it once and set it down. Second time it's going through. It's in your lap. Trust me. When I first started flying I used to puke as soon as I walked on the airplane. Just to get it over with. Just a psychological thing. I was gonna go somewhere. Oh, the knot-heads in Washington. They were so embarrassed about it that they did award our crew. Now out of seven squadrons that were deployed worldwide, I think it was seven, twelve crews per squadron, we were awarded crew of the quarter for that mission there.

BOC: That's pretty substantial.

GM: Yeah. But they couldn't tell us why, because the knot-heads in Washington were so embarrassed everything about the mission was classified. We didn't know then what we know now, of course—the spy case with John Walker. He had shared where those lines were. That was part of what he shared.

BOC: So this was about testing that end, kind of jerking you around.

GM: And it cost billions of dollars for that encounter.

BOC: There must have been a little chuckle on the Soviets' part that this old clunker boat is causing all this.

GM: Well there may or may not have been. Now don't underestimate the effectiveness of a hidden-class or a level-one-class nuclear submarine. They're shooting.

BOC: It's still a nuclear submarine.

GM: They could take out a carrier fleet <finger snap evident on audiotape> like that. That's their job. Old and raspy and antiquated technology, but very effective. I can take a single-shot .22 and kill anybody I want to. One time. I just need to be a good shot.

[End of tape side A. GM was talking while thunder rumbled, so we had not noticed that the tape had stopped until a few minutes had passed. GM goes on to explain that old and simple missile technology was still frighteningly dangerous.]

...but later on, technology continued to go. I mean, you gotta think. When this technology was going on ... we flew around in the dark and would light up the world to see if we could find the submarine. Hello! [GM later explained he was making a comment on how very primitive the search technology was in his early days.] We did other things like hang a big scoop out the airplane, and we'd scoop up particles of the air and then we'd inspect it to see if there was any diesel exhaust in it.

BOC: Seems like a reasonable idea.

GM: Well, yeah, they're trying to do that with nuclear particles in the ocean now too. That's the new technology, or new stupidity. I don't know. I'm not sure which is which. But from that [old way of] finding submarines to where we've evolved [to]—[from] when I got involved in it, [to] the latest and greatest thing—with the plasmatic computerized touch stuff happens.

But they got away from the learning, the teaching that I got from Donny Ray Perkins and Tommy Davis, and Guy Whitely. And they got in all this technology stuff. I mean the three-dimensional videos start picking the submarine and turning it all around and this is that. That's all good. But it's in the book. You [have to] get on top. You learn here. What I did talk them into doing was taking recordings of contacts. Digitally enhance it. Put it on CD. Bring it to computers and show them what this guy is doing. In the old days what I used to have to do was take a piece of paper, lay it down, take up multipoint dividers and go: "Okay, this is a submarine, this is a submarine, this is a submarine, this is a submarine." But they never told me why. What I tried to do as I departed was go tell the student what situation the submarine was in. Don't always give him the closest point of approach. Don't drive him through a barrier where he's only got a mile on each side, or a half a mile on each side and give him the perfect situation and say: "That's a submarine." That's not a submarine. I mean it is, but you're not going to get him like that, not very often. You get your look and a sight and cross hairs and you're lucky. You're lucky if you ever get that.

BOC: I was reading a book by a guy who used to be a big game hunter and now he leads wildlife photography treks. And he said almost exactly that same thing. He said if you spend half an hour finding one track and then a half an hour finding another track, you'll know a lot about those two tracks. If you spend time getting to know the animal in it's environment, you'll end up where the animal is going to be.

GM: Perfect. Early on we talked about [how] I had this great success with my initial flight and I was subsequently successful after that and hot and all kinds of stuff. And then I was kind of shit canned because of that incident with the young officer, but that was my—I didn't know it at the time, of course—but that was my foundation; because it was required for me in order to be able to write those lessons, there was so

much research done and I absorbed stuff, that the next time I was challenged...

BOC: It was background.

GM: It's like wait, you start with an empty toolbox. If you throw
enough tools in it over the years, you just reach down and go: "Yeah, I
got one of those. I need that."[5] And there were other incidents. I had to
tap-dance in front of a commanding officer more than once.

It's true. I was a brand-new chief. I retired as a chief petty officer.
But I was brand spanking new. My khakis had not been to the cleaners
a second time. We had a mission that was really important. It's an
evaluation of the squadron. They put one of our submarines out there,
which I never understood anyway. If we can't catch our submarines,
then hey, we've got some really good submarines! Why are you chew-
ing my ass? Those guys are doing their job. But they were sent out to
simulate a Soviet submarine.

And I came to work and the crew just landed and a kid came in,
one of my kids, young people, came in and said: "Gary Mac, I cannot
believe it. I had him. I had him. I had him. I had him." I'm going:
"That's all good news, except the 'd' part; I'd rather have a 've' on the
end of that. What happened?" And he goes: "The TACCO and the pilot
talked me out of it and went off and looked in another direction." And I
just hung my head. And it was not five minutes after that kid came in
that the skipper called and said: "Chief Mac, can you come up to my
office and talk to me?" And he just rolled out the mission and said:
"What the hell happened and how come we didn't get this submarine?"
And they're all blaming that kid. I said: "Skipper, he's here, he's here,
he's here, he's here. The kid logged everything. It's all written down.
I'll have to go to the wing and listen to the tape and look at the computer replay."

And I went over there and listened to it and, sure as I'm sitting
here, that full commander wanting a promotion, and that full lieutenant
commander wanting promotion off of this evaluative flight talked that
kid out of chasing that submarine. They didn't trust him because of his
lower rank, although he was excellent. I certified him personally. And
they're going: "If you certified him, it must be your fault." No. But
they talked him out of it. And that had happened to me so many times,
so many times. It was flipping my head around. And while I was listening to the oral tape, the communication tape on the airplane over at the
wing, the executive officer, soon to be commanding officer, came in

and he says, "Chief what is it?" I said: "It's right here" and I just
wound it back and played it for him. You could hear the kid arguing his
case. You heard the tactical officer, the lieutenant officer overriding.
And you heard the pilot, full commander, overriding. I mean what's a
third class supposed to do? You all know what you're doing. You can
fly the plane. It's just my job to catch a submarine. I've been through
that so many times.

BOC: It's such a typical thing in movies too.

GM: And in life. The little guy sometimes knows. The squeaky wheel
gets the oil. This is not the first go-round that got stuck. I felt so bad for
that kid. I went back and the XO beat me back to the hangar and went
into the skipper and talked. And I went straight to the skipper's office,
and in the skipper's office was that pilot and tactical coordinator. We
talked about this, and I just said: "It's March. I'm retiring in June. It
takes a congressional act to get me demoted now. I'm gonna speak my
piece." And I told him straight out. I waited my turn. The skipper said:
"Chief McAlister, what have you got to say about this?" I just turned to
him and said: "If any one of your officers ever talks my operators out
of a call again, I just don't know what I'll do. I'll quit."
    I said: "You guys cannot chase a submarine from the front end of
that airplane. It cannot be done. You're welcome to walk down that
tube and assume that seat. I'm gratified that you've read the books and
you know the signatures, and you know what different submarines do
and what their equipments is, and what they look like in shadows. And
all that kind of stuff. But you cannot catch one from the pilot's seat. It
cannot be done. It never has been. It never will be. Not until they move
all of this computerized gear up there in that cockpit and you put two
AWs up there with it. They don't call us AWs for nothing. Antisubmarine Warfare Systems Operators. It just cannot be done." And I was just
inflamed with this guy. And then the room just got really silent.
    The skipper just kind of looked up and kind of looked around the
room and looked at me and said: "Chief, thank you for your time."
And, I think, he said to close the door on the way out. And as I was
closing the door, I heard him scream, literally scream: "Do any of you
understand what Chief McAlister just said?" And I just kind of yanked
the door and walked off. I had a little pep in my step. Now we're talking four hundred yards from his office to my office, maybe two hundred yards. It was a long ways, a big-ass hangar. These are not small
airplanes. I don't know if you noticed. Anyway down to my office, and

then I got on that kid. I got him and I got this great big tall Tennessee kid, and I got right in his face. I said: "Bobby if you ever, ever let an officer talk you out of a call again, I'll knock you out. I'll knock you out. That's your job and you protect it with every ounce of integrity that you've got. Because if you can't be trusted or if you waiver on a call or if you ever say 'No sir, I don't think it's him' because somebody else said that, then you're no good."

BOC: Tell me something, when you're sitting there what do you have?

GM: Equipment-wise?

BOC: Yeah.

GM: We call it "dirty gray paper." It's an electrograph kind of stuff, takes the noise out of the water in a microphone. Radiographics sends it back to the airplane and sorts it out. But that's not all of it. I can also hear that stuff. I've got a diode that I can [tune and aim] listen to sound and go: "Yeah, it's a whale over there. They're having a good time. Over here's a dolphin." You know, I can electronically move around to different parts of the ocean. That kind of stuff. It's just a graph that labels frequencies at different spectrums. From zero to forever.

Everything makes noise. Now sporadic noise like these sparrows [points to birds eating crumbs under the roof], it might not be recorded. It might come up as specks. We call it fly shit in the pepper. It's just black on black. It wouldn't matter. But machinery, it's very specific. It functions in a specific way. So if you study that long enough, you know that certain machinery functions a certain way. And if you change it, the anomaly, like a diesel submarine, if it's running along sucking air, running its diesel engines, and then it goes below the water, what's going to happen? Well, they can't run those diesel engines on water. So they turn them off. Anyway, [the sound] changes.

Now this is a scary thought, and this is just my philosophy as an old sailor; we did away with all of our diesel submarines years ago. I think the Grey Back was the last one to go. And I caught that, too, ha ha. It was just—I watched her [the submarine], watched her, watched her, watched her, watched her … gotcha! He [the captain] ran on his things and turned them off and just said this line has never been there before. There's the anomaly. One little tiny speck, and everything went totally blank. Engines are gone. Got nothing but ocean, except for that, and I got him. But anyway, we need to go back to diesel boats. They're quieter. They're as fast now with our new technology in batteries. They can stay submerged for days. It's cheaper than nuclear. We don't have a [good way to store nuclear waste]. What do you do with a nuclear core? It used to be: What do you do with a drunken sailor? Now it's: What do you do with a nuclear core? They're good boats. Other countries are doing it. We're gonna be behind the curve if we don't get involved.

BOC: Two things especially interest me in all the stuff you are saying. One, if you substitute a few nouns and verbs in there, you could be giving the talk I try to give to new doc students that the only way you can be a doctor of something is total immersion in it. You have to know all the stuff in the toolbox. You have to know enough to know the anomalies. And you have to have that passion of life. "I've got that sucker." It's the same thing whether it's a submarine or it's a problem in quantum physics. You have to be pretty damn happy that this is the way you are spending your life and you get those moments.

GM: I think you'll enjoy my tape [video of farewell ceremony]. It starts off with the Navy band playing, but you have to be somebody to get the Navy band to play.

BOC: Well sure, they don't just play for anybody.

GM: That's right. And then there's the idiots, and you'll see them, the officers that I talked about; they're idiots. They're more worried about where they're going with their career than they were about doing the job at hand. Do the job at all cost. You don't win a horse race by staying in the pasture.

BOC: Or placing fourth or fifth but looking nice.

GM: Well, there you are. You're right with me on your statement. But watch [the video]. Here's the guy that wrote the speech and can't read it. Now my speech, I stutter and stammer at times, but I was emotional. I'm kissing it good-bye here. But watch it. They're reading from a script and can't read it.

If I could go back and fly again today, if they said: "We got a wild one, we don't know where he is, we need you, we'd like your advice"—my wife would have to get a taxi from Dallas tomorrow, because I'd be gone. I'd go do it right now. And you know, I believe I could with minimal, minimal amount [of preparation].

BOC: You might need to work on puking right at first.

GM: Right, I might have to puke first. I'd probably shit my pants. We used to have a crew, I loved them. It wasn't my crew. I wish it had been. I wish I'd thought it up. It was crew seven or ten—it was crew ten that said: "Flexible is too stiff." And it had a harpoon missile that was bent over like a limp dick or something. Flexible is too stiff. I'll never forget that because if you're just going to go with the flow then that's where you are. If you're going to be successful, then you better reach out and grab as the flow goes by. Reach for that brass ring and stuff. I don't know why I share all this stuff. I liked you when I met you on the train.

BOC: But I think that's important. It goes back to the searching stuff and it's part of what I'm trying to get at in the book. So many people get the book knowledge you were talking about gaining but that's all they have. Or they have one piece of experience. But it's this odd juggling between having to know a whole shit load of stuff really well and know its patterns.

GM: I could not get advanced [in rank] because of the amount of books that I had to read. There were volumes of stuff with very obscure questions. Hidden questions. Questions that had been on the tests year after year after year. Finally, and I pay tribute to this boy in my video, he just said: "It's your turn. You have to make chief this year. We cannot function without you." He told me [I had to do it]. He was my roommate. He kept me up hours late at night. Gobs of hours, just flipping cards [psyching me up by pretending he was me and] going: "I've done this study, I've read it. I read it. I know I read faster than you. You're the best there ever was." He just laid gobs of praise on me. I love him to death, John Rudolf. All of that meant nothing other than getting in front of the committee that was going to promote. That's all that means. It didn't catch a single submarine. It's just stuff that people wrote down saying: "If you don't know where it is, you can't find it."

BOC: I'm enthralled with the way you tell your story. It sounds just like the bounty hunter I've interviewed. In that, there's this constant juggling, this constant interplay between knowing the big picture and looking for that little anomaly, the thing that is out of place, but it's out of place in a way that does not makes sense, but it's out of place in a way that makes it observable to you as something different from…

GM: …not noticed by anyone else, not even visible sometimes to anyone else. I don't mean to pile gobs of praise upon myself. I'm just barely settling in with the fact that I was pretty good. I watched my retirement tape last night maybe three times and I'm going: "Boy if I could just x that out. That's just too much. Just x that part out." But I can't. It's history. It's part of it. But there were others like Tommy Davis and Donny Ray Perkins, and we used to [do] stuff that [was] supposedly illegal. We operated under rules. Okay, no electronic emissions. You can't use your radar. You can't use your IFF. You can't use your identification printer file. I don't know if you know all of this. You can't use your intercom, emissions, nothing. Nothing electronic goes out of the airplane. Well that's so stupid, because you got your radar altimeter working. Hello? They'd say all this stuff. But in the old days, before all this technology, we used to have a variance radar which you could bring up. You could turn the transmitter on and you could just barely bring it on, just turn it up just a little bit. Just a tiny, tiny emission. Not very strong at all. Man if you got anything it was lucky, and then you could also change it so only the rear radar would come on and it worked at a different frequency so you could turn it up and the submarine thinks you're running away at the same time you're running in right on top of him. And they're going: "Okay, we can go ahead and surface now because the airplane is flying away." Not! We gotcha!

So I called Dean Norman up on my handset. In fact, we even got to where we had a crew ball. It was like a little rubber soccer ball with a big 8 on it. We'd roll it up and down the hallway so we wouldn't put it on the tape because we knew it would be illegal. He'd throw it at me or I'd throw it at him and say I need a [made-up name] and he'd bring his radar up just a tiny bit, just enough to see if there's anything out there. He goes: "Nothing there." I said: "Okay, we're going the other way. Okay, TACCO, fly around, come back to this buoy. And come back to get it done." But that was the mission.

In the old days they used to grade us. I never understood this grading system. If you got an eighty-five that was a hundred. Give me a hundred, or give me eighty-five, I don't care. Eighty-five was a perfect score. I never understood it. It was extremely complicated, and they would grade everybody. And that's why so many postflights would take sometimes an hour to put the airplane away, and then four or five hours to sit there and have your brains beat out after a ten- or twelve-hour flight and a three-hour preflight. Preflight took three hours. And brief usually took about an hour. So it's a twenty-four-hour day doing this stuff. If you were lucky it was three or four hours to get to where you had to be, so you could get some sleep, if you could sleep on a four-engine turbo prop. I could. I'd hop out of the seat and just go to sleep. I had horrible dreams always about falling out of the sky.

But the scores, they finally did away with that. My initial catch, the very lucky one that said you're the man, the very initial one I wrote down, it was a nuclear submarine and it was in a turbine converting to an electric motor situation. And I wrote that down. That's all I wrote down. Then I jumped on him. I stayed with him. I never lost him. I was a puppy. There was a senior operator next to me. He denied the call, called him off, but I stayed with him. We got back. The call [that] had been sent back said "may have" a type one submarine out here in the Sea of Japan that they didn't know was there.

That's what the big thing was. No one knew he was there. They hadn't seen him leave ports—satellites and all that. He may not be there ... anyway. But my brief was: "Keep your eyes open; you might be surprised." I remember that so specifically. Keep your eyes open; you might be surprised. We were going down looking for a submarine tender. And I'm looking at this going: "Hello? Hello? Hello?" This was two minutes on my brain. "Hello? Hello? Hello? Yo boss, hello?" "Ah don't worry about it." "Shaft rate. ... Hello?" And it just didn't make sense, but that was the one that wasn't. But do you know what I got for a grade that night? Zero. I was the hero with the zero.

Because I didn't keep writing down what I saw, was denied by the supposed authority, refused by the pilots, the intelligentsia of the crew, but I knew what I had. And they just went: "Mac that's so great! That's a great call! That's a good call! Here's your grade: F, because you didn't write it down." I have a problem with that, I don't know. That was fun. I enjoyed northern Japan. And I enjoyed my retirement. I hope you enjoy the tape. The ceremony, the first part is the idiots, alright, with the band playing. But the first part is the idiots reading a whole bunch of stuff about me. And then there's seven minutes of me and then there's a few minutes of sailors on liberty after standing at the beer keg, slamming down the whatevers. And the secretary's very shaky.

In the old one [cruise book], the VP47 book, the brown one, there's a picture of us where we're getting ready to rescue some people that were in a capsized ship and there's a patch that's a four; I don't have a pen; that's alright. [GM draws design with his finger on table top.] It's a circle like this and it's got a four but it's a screw that goes through it. We were the screw four. And they hated that thing. I designed it. I propagated it. I paid for the patches and the crew put them on. But what happened was that we did some grade A SW [submarine warfare.] It was after that grade, I got a zero and the rest of the crew didn't get much more. The whole thing was that it was a [supposedly] failed mission but we found the submarine. I don't understand that. So I designed that [patch]. Gosh, this was a long time ago, '76? [That's] when the Japanese were gonna buy this airplane, the P3, and they invited our crew down to come because they were involved in that search as well, with older-style airplanes. They invited our crew down to do cherry festival and we were gonna swap crews. Let them fly our airplane and us go fly on their airplane. Scary idea. Scary. But anyway, the admiral sent us a case of scotch in a nice wooden case with compliments and everything. We painted a screw four on it and before the C-130 [transport plane] left slid it right back on the C-130 saying we got plenty of scotch and we don't need your compliments.

We could find a submarine anytime. It wasn't the best move we ever made, but we can brag about it today. Wes Burd, Brendon Martin, those guys are telling the same story today that I'm telling right now. It's that level of difference, that we knew we did it, we had it right.[6]

Epilogue

Janes (1989) studied strategic methods of submarine maneuvers and applied military search tactics to information search planning. Just as Gary McAlister had stressed, Janes asserts that intuitive searchers are successful searchers. Janes and McAlister also shared the idea that studying ocean currents and knowing the hyperdimensional conceptual search space lowers the cost-to-gain ratio by personalizing the organization of the space. These studies remain true to the hunter-gatherer need for spatial and tactile experiences.

Following are the main points of the Janes search model noted by Jodi Kearns while reading Janes's dissertation "Toward a Search Theory of Information":

1. It is a hyperdimensional conceptual space.
2. The space is continuous, and can be treated as discrete (organized in terms of cells).
3. The space is universal but individual (the same documents and representations exist for all people, but we each organize them differently). Gary McAlister's organization of the same information seems to minimize entropy, especially when compared with the organization of the other submarine chasers and crews.
4. Two types of dimensions organize the space: intellectual and functional.
5. There will be empty cells, corresponding to documents not yet created.
6. Effort and target distribution are discrete.
7. There are two stages of effort:
   a. Stage 1 is system's (obtaining retrieval set).
   b. Stage 2 is user's (evaluating).

Page 148 describes submarine as document.

And my very favorite point: Just as Gary McAlister described, intuition is part of this model. Searchers must be intuitive to be successful (p. 157). Overall, I can just say, "Yup, it's exactly what Gary Mac said."

Chapter 4

Fifty-Two Stories to an Arrest: Bounty Hunting

Brian O'Connor

The brother of author Brian O'Connor has considerable experience as a bounty hunter. He is Ivy League educated, a jewelry designer, and instructor in rescue techniques. He has frequently discussed the foundations of his investigative work. Information gathering and analysis are the primary aspects of the task. Knowledge of criminal behavior patterns together with "observation of trifles" (to paraphrase Sherlock Holmes) are significant in determining what sorts of information to gather, as well as how to proceed with analysis. The importance of bounty hunting for our book is the active nature of the goal—that is, the information is not simply waiting to be found. This takes us out of the realm within which so much library and database service takes place—an assumption that if the patron can just describe the need, there is a tidy, preexisting answer package.

Bounty hunters (also known as skip tracers or recovery agents) operate within an old Anglo-American tradition. Since there is a concept of *innocent until proven guilty*, a judge is empowered to let an accused person stay free so long as there is some assurance the person will return for trial. That assurance is often in the form of a monetary bond. When the accused cannot afford the bond, a third-party bail bond agent can put up the required funds. If the accused *skips* before trial, then the bond agency stands to lose the bond money. At this point a bond agency will often hire a bounty hunter.

Generally, a bounty hunter receives a percentage of the bond for returning the accused. Usually payment is made only for the actual return or presentation of a death certificate, thus, the bounty hunter works on speculation. While there is some controversy over the powers of bounty hunters, they do not operate simply as remnants of the Old West.

Bail bondsmen and bounty hunters serve an important sup-
plemental role in state law enforcement efforts. After an arrest but before trial, most defendants hire bail bondsmen to
post a bond with the court in order to secure the defendant's release. The state then gives the bondsman legal custody of the defendant, and provides that the bond will be
forfeited if the defendant fails to return to court. Bondsmen
seeking defendants who either have fled or have missed a
court date generally employ bounty hunters who, as agents
of bondsmen, are vested with the bondsmen's powers.
These bounty hunters are generally considered to have the
power to search for and arrest a defendant on bond similar
to those of a law enforcement official pursuing an escaped
prisoner. Thus, bounty hunters need not obtain arrest or
search warrants, need not "knock and announce" before
searching, and need not seek formal extradition of captured
defendants.

The broad powers of bounty hunters to search and arrest a defendant on bond generally arise from common law,
and the powers are considered to be derived from the bail
bondsman's contract with the defendant. (Canady, 2000)

This relationship is given substance in a Supreme Court ruling in
Taylor v. Taintor (1872)

When bail is given, the principal is regarded as delivered to
the custody of his sureties. Their dominion is a continuance
of the original imprisonment. Whenever they choose to do
so, they may seize him and deliver him up in their dis-
charge; and if that cannot be done at once, they may im-
prison him until it can be done. They may exercise their
rights in person or by agent. They may pursue him into another State; may arrest him on the Sabbath; and, if necessary, may break and enter his house for that purpose. The
seizure is not made by virtue of new process. None is
needed. It is likened to the rearrest by the sheriff of an es-
caping prisoner.

Patrick notes, in his examination of bounty hunters' legal standing in
light of high profile "mistakes" by bounty hunters:

Constitutional protections are applicable only against the
government and "state actors." Bounty hunters have long
been recognized by the courts as private actors, and thus
immune from constitutional restraints. Consequently, while

bounty hunters do enjoy police-like powers—courts have held that they may conduct nonconsensual searches and use reasonable force in arresting defendants—they are not restricted in their tactics in the same manner as state agents. Specifically, they are free from the strictures of the Fourth, Fifth, and Sixth Amendments, as well as the relevant sections of the U.S. Code. Thus, bounty hunters may conduct warrantless searches and arrests and pursue a defendant beyond state lines....[However,] bounty hunters are not completely unfettered by the law. To the contrary, the bail bond industry is bound by the threat of criminal sanction, notions of reasonable force, and other principles of tort law. Indeed, very few bounty hunters employ the kind of spectacular violence reported by the media. More typical is the use of psychological warfare—bounty hunters employing various forms of deception and seduction in the apprehension of fugitives. (Patrick, 1999, pp. 171-172)

Figures from the National Association of Bail Enforcement Agents (NABEA) suggest that only a small percentage of accused skip and only a small percentage of those have used a bond agency. Even so, the number of skips sought by bounty hunters is about thirty thousand per year.

The story of a single case, constructed from the daily notes kept during the investigation (which might, at any time, be taking place concurrently with one or more unrelated cases), gives substance to Bates's (1989b) term *evolving search* described as follows: "Each new piece of information they encounter gives them new ideas and directions to follow and, consequently, a new conception of the query. At each stage they are not just modifying the search terms used in order to get a better match for a single query. Rather the query itself (as well as the search terms used) is continually shifting, in part or whole" (p. 408).

TO: FIRE DEPARTMENT PERSONNEL
                 FIRE EQUIPMENT SUPPLY COMPANIES
FROM: David O'Connor, Investigator

I am in charge of an investigation to apprehend an individual
wanted in several states. A personality trait of this individual is
FASCINATION with the Fire Service and associated equipment.
He has been observed at the scene of several fires in the New England area impersonating Fire Fighters (especially officers). He has
also been seen with fire equipment in his car (hats, bunker jackets,
uniforms, etc.). To this point there is NO reason to suspect any
involvement in arson. He likes to hang out around fire stations and
socialize, usually stating that he was/is involved in the Fire Service
in some manner.

This individual has MANY identities and IDs from around the
country. He can also convince almost anyone of almost anything.
His vital statistics are as follows:

Real name: ANTHONY CARUSO
Race: CAUCASIAN
Height: 6' 2"
Weight: PROBABLY AROUND 240 lbs.
Other: USUALLY HAS WHITE HAIR AND A
                 WHITE CHIN BEARD BUT MAY
                 HAVE FULL BEARD OR BE CLEAN
                 SHAVEN. COMPLEXION MAY BE
                 CRATERED. LARGE SCARS ON
                 STOMACH, TOP OF HEAD, LEFT OF
                 CENTER AT HAIRLINE

If you see this individual, please take NO action yourself.
Try to get a license plate number and description of his vehicle.
If you are convinced that he is the subject in question and time
permits, call your local Police Department and have them check
him out. **GIVE THIS LETTER TO THE OFFICERS WHO
CHECK HIM OUT.**

I WILL PICK HIM UP

Case Report

Note: In the following account, names have been changed and identifying data deleted (indicated by the use of brackets containing all upper case letters).

On November 17, 1989, I received a call from Dennis Bail Bonds in Chester, New Hampshire. They inquired as to whether I would be interested in taking a contract to find an individual. I stated that I was.

I went to Chester to pick up the appropriate paperwork and discuss pertinent particulars. The individual was one Anthony Caruso, DOB 10/05/44. Reason for location was revocation of bail that was posted for the subject at Belknap Superior Court. I was informed that the bail bond was in the amount of $50,000.00 and was issued by a Mr. Ed Brown. Information was relatively sparse:

- Eyes: brown
- Hair: gray
- SS no.: [SOCIAL SECURITY NUMBER]
- Credit ref.: Eileen Caruso (ex-wife)
  Tampa, Florida
- Mother: Marguerite Caruso,
  Stoneham, Massachusetts
- Sister: Mrs. Robert Jones
  [STREET ADDRESS]
  Stoneham, Massachusetts
- Brother-in-law: Robert Jones, same address as above
- Girlfriend (?): Claudette Pelton/Pellerin
  Rochester/Gonic area?

Our first steps were to locate the possible girlfriend and call Robert Jones, Anthony's brother-in-law. My contacts found that there was no reasonable possibility by the name of Claudette Pelton in the area. I ran the name Pellerin through the computers and found a Claudette Pellerin with an address of [STREET ADDRESS] New Castle, New Hampshire 03854. Her DOB [DATE OF BIRTH] made her a strong possibility.

Then, I called Robert Jones on the phone. He was very cooperative. He and his wife live at [STREET ADDRESS] in Stoneham, Massachusetts. The house is owned by Mrs. Marguerite Caruso, Anthony's mother. When bail was posted, Anthony's mother used the house as collateral to guarantee the bail bond. Robert Jones stated that the house was "supposed to be his and his wife's." When Marguerite's husband died, the house was "supposed to be signed over" to Robert and his wife. In an effort to "delay the pain of the paperwork," time passed and the house was never signed over. Robert also loaned the 10 percent needed to secure the bond. In short, he has a tremendous amount to lose if the bail bond ends up forfeited.

Over the phone, I learned the following about the current situation:

- Robert Jones despises Anthony Caruso.
- Anthony Caruso has a long record of trouble, usually in the form of bad checks, bank fraud, confidence schemes, misrepresentation. A check of local police records even indicated a bad check arrest back in the middle 1970s.
- Approximately fourteen years ago, Anthony did time in Danbury Prison, apparently for bank fraud.
- After his arrest in New Hampshire for violation of the controlled drug act, he was sent to Belknap County House of Correction. He made many phone calls from that institution and charged them to Robert Jones's phone.
- Anthony got out of jail around October 13, 1989. On October 25, Anthony showed up at the house. He and his mother then disappeared until October 29. They are believed to have gone to New York City.
- On October 31, Anthony called the house. Robert had words with him about the phone bill (now near $675). They hung up on bad terms. On November 2, Anthony called to apologize.
- A couple of days later, while the family was having breakfast, Anthony came in. He made a gesture to Robert. He then made a production of showing a receipt from New England Telephone saying that he had paid $600 on the phone bill. After he left, Robert found out that the receipt was a fake.

I made an appointment for myself and my assistant, LS, to meet with Robert on the night of November 18 at the Reading Fire Department where he is employed as a firefighter.

Later that same night (Friday, November 17) I took a ride to New Castle, New Hampshire. I went to the address I had for Claudette to observe the house and neighborhood: upper-class residential, no sign of activity, and since there was no immediate indicator of presence, we did not establish surveillance.

The next morning, I went to the New Castle Police Department and asked if they were familiar with either Claudette Pellerin or Anthony Caruso. They were not. When asked about the address I had, they said that the house was owned by Mr. and Mrs. Sawyer. I then went to the post office and inquired. I found that Claudette Pellerin had indeed received mail there, but she had moved about a year ago. Her forwarding address was: [STREET ADDRESS] Delray Beach, Florida.

My next action was to return to [house owned by Sawyers]. I knocked on the door and Mr. Sawyer answered. I told him I represented an insurance company and we were trying to locate Claudette. He said she had not lived there for about a year, but that his wife and she were good friends and kept in touch with each other. He asked that I leave my name and number and he would have his wife pass on the message. I did and left.

Sunday night, we met Robert Jones for two-and-a-half hours. He passed on the following information:

- When Anthony was at the house in October, he was driving a 1989 Buick Park Avenue with Massachusetts plates. Unknown registration.
- There was a good chance that when Anthony and his mother went to New York they stayed at Anthony's old address: Royalton Hotel.
- (As mentioned before, Anthony had a Rochester police card that went back to the early/mid-1970s. The address he used at that time was this Royalton Hotel.)
- Royalton Hotel is where Anthony was arrested by FBI in the 1970s.
- Anthony had a habit of using other people's or false/stolen credit cards. His mother's card had recently seen over $600 of his charge activity. He probably had a Discover Card and a Visa out of the Chase Manhattan Bank.
- He uses the aliases of: Buddy Caruso, Bob Hayes, Anthony Coleman, Anthony Bocco.
- At one time he and his ex-wife, Eileen, lived in Laconia, New Hampshire, next to the [COMPANY NAME] amusement center. He spent a great deal of time in the Laconia, Tilton, Gilmanton, Weirs Beach area.

- Ogunquit Beach was also favorite haunt; in fact, when he was arrested last, he was at Ogunquit.
- Past and present contacts might include: [list of seven people, only two of whom appear herein]
- Habits and patterns:
    o Very close to mother (so he can use her)
    o Stays in touch with mother
    o If pulling a scam in an area, will probably be working at a high-end auto sales center
    o To this point has been very consistent
    o Swings between New York, Portsmouth [New Hampshire], Maine coast areas, Florida
    o Will use anybody for his personal gain
    o Will feign a disease such as cancer
- After the November 3 blowout over the phone bills, Robert had the phone company put a charge/collect block on the line. This ended ability to review activity on the monthly phone bills.

For the week leading up to Thanksgiving our investigation centered around the New England area. From his past patterning, we felt that he might try to contact his mother during the holiday. Surveillance was established. **No physical contact attempts**.

This was a definite break in his past consistency. Perhaps the knowledge that his court hearing was on November 27 and he had no intention of showing up made him consider making himself scarce.

After the Thanksgiving weekend, we decided we would be aggressive on all possible contacts (we hadn't done that in the previous week for fear of scaring him off from his probable meet with his mother). To this point, all contacts with friends, family, or possible associates had been noninvestigator in nature. Again, the reason was that we felt Anthony might feel secure that he had not yet violated bail conditions and might continue usual patterns of contact. Identifying ourselves as investigators might have tipped our hand.

The week after Thanksgiving saw the following activity:

- I contacted all police departments in areas that Anthony was known to frequent in the New Hampshire, Massachusetts, and Maine areas. No contacts or sightings were found.
- I spoke with Trooper Burgess of the New Hampshire State Police, who was involved in the controlled-drug violation investigation and arrest. She told me that:

- o   Anthony was a real con artist,
- o   he would probably resist arrest (he had bitten an officer during the New Hampshire contact),
- o   he would try to talk his way out of apprehension,
- o   had no friends in the New Hampshire law enforcement or legal system,
- o   rumor was that he had been traveling with a woman who might have had kids with her. Janice?

- On Monday morning there was a message on my answering machine from Claudette Pellerin. She was responding to the message left with the Sawyers and inquiring as to the nature of the contact (again, I had not revealed the real reason for the contact to the Sawyers). I did not call her back at this time due to my uncertainty as to her involvement.
- My assistant, LS, called the Royalton Hotel (in a noninvestigator context) and found that there was no recent record of Anthony being there. The hotel also did not know how he might be contacted.
- On Monday night, I received a call from Robert Jones. He was in Portsmouth, New Hampshire, following up on a lead that would probably tell us where Anthony was. When he called me back at about 11:00 p.m., he stated that his sources (credible but confidential) stated that Anthony was in Florida.
- I called Mr. Brian Dennis and Mr. Brown to inform them of the report and keep them up-to-date on our investigation. We collectively decided to center the investigation on the possibility of Anthony's presence in Florida.
- I then evaluated where we were. I believed that I had to be very careful in how I approached the Florida investigation. I could either go to Florida or conduct the investigation from here. Mr. Brown proposed that we do the latter for the time being. It would be extremely easy to tip Mr. Caruso off that we were looking for him in a serious way. I therefore decide to limit my contacts to "friendly" contacts until more information was gathered.
- LS called Eileen Caruso, Anthony's ex-wife. She owns her own business in the Tampa area. In a nutshell, Anthony had burned her badly. He had taken her for about $40,000. She was working hard to pay back the debts he had left her with and figured that she only had about $9,000 left to go.
- Eileen Caruso was very cooperative. She told us the following:
- o   She had not seen or heard from Anthony lately.

- He had made contact by phone shortly after he had gotten out of jail in October.
- He tried to see if she was interested in getting back together.
- Needless to say, she was not and told him so in no uncertain terms. She told him where to go.
- Eileen, like most people, despises him.
- Eileen had lived with him in a chalet in the Laconia region during the 1975–1976 period.
- Janice (the other woman) had flaunted herself and her relationship with Anthony. She ended up wearing Eileen's jewelry and possessing many of her belongings. Eileen did not know much about her except that she was a heavy drinker and loved to party. She also had two children.
- Eileen explained that Anthony swung between older and younger women. When he was with an older woman (as we will see with Claudette) he would go for long periods of time following the straight and narrow and getting into no trouble. Then he would get involved with a younger woman (as Janice) and go off the deep end.
- Anthony had run up credit card bills of close to $800 in the [COMPANY NAME] Liquor Stores. Anthony is not that heavy a drinker, so this may be related to a second party, possibly someone like Janice.
- Anthony loved good, high-priced restaurants. A haunt was the [NAME] on Sanibel Island in Florida.
- Eileen stated it would be possible that Anthony would spend time with two or three women in Florida by bouncing back and forth.
- May of 1989, Anthony had charged $60 at a restaurant in Palm Beach called [NAME].
- Eileen was cautious, at first, about talking with us because Anthony (or an associate) was known to call her and other people under false pretext to obtain information he could use to his benefit.
- She would gladly call us if she heard anything, and hoped that if we found him we would "save a piece for her."

I learned that Janice went by the name of [DELETED] and had two children. Her father lived in Tampa, Florida. He was reported to be a friendly contact, so I called. He, too, hated Anthony and hoped that we found him. He could not offer much information. Anthony, he felt, was a terrible influence on Janice's life. When I asked where Janice lived, he said he did not know. I believe that he does know, but is showing some protection of his daughter.

I believe it was on Wednesday night that I received a phone call from Mr. Robert Jones stating his contacts (confidential) had two definite sightings of Anthony in Florida. Both [SIGHTING LOCATIONS] are not far from [STREET ADDRESS] where Janice's parents live.

I called Mr. Brown to inform him of the report by Mr. Jones. I then called the County Sheriff's Department in Tampa. It was late at night and I could only talk with the computer department. I asked them to check the record on Anthony and see if there was any current paperwork on him. They stated that there were three definite warrants standing (robbery, grand theft second degree, and grand theft auto), and it looked like there were two more from another county that they couldn't quite figure out at the late hour. I also learned from a contact that Anthony is believed to have an aunt in Florida, possibly P. Clark in Holiday, Florida.

Next day, I talked to Brian Dennis about the situation. There was a lot of evidence indicating that Anthony might well be in the Tampa/Palm Beach areas. Brian contacted Mr. Brown. We decided to contract a Florida group to investigate the situation. Next day, I contacted Katie's Bail Bonds out of Tampa. This group had posted a bail bond for Anthony in the past (which he had jumped). They recommended Frank Quato of Frank Quato Bail Bonds also of Tampa. Mr. Quato indicated that he was familiar with Anthony and would take the case.

Two nights later, I received another call from Robert Jones stating that there had been another sighting in the [SAME FLORIDA] area. I passed the information to Mr. Quato. A call from Robert the next night indicated that his sources indicated a possible link with Claudette and that she should be watched. I passed the information on to Mr. Quato.

Discussions with Mr. Brown and Mr. Dennis led to the decision to look into the Sawyer/Claudette connection more closely. I returned to the Sawyer residence and told them I was an investigator looking for Anthony Caruso. They sat down with me as I explained who Anthony was and the possible connection with Claudette. All of a sudden, Mrs. Sawyer said, "Wait a minute, I wonder if that could be Tony?"

The story unfolds:

• Mrs. Sawyer met Claudette in the mid 1970s when they were both working at a radio station in Portsmouth, New Hampshire.

- Once, Claudette told her the story of a man named Tony she had been involved with. He was dashing and wined and dined her. He would take her to the best stores and tell her to buy whatever she liked. They traveled and lived the high life.
- Claudette had two (I believe) children at the time who she all but gave up for the good life.
- After a while, she became suspicious about the fact that Tony never introduced her to his friends, never told her what he did, and received very secretive phone calls.
- Once, she returned to where they lived and found the place cleaned out and the mattresses sliced up.
- Things deteriorated from there.
- While out for a ride (on a trip?) one day, when Tony got out of the car for something, she got behind the wheel and [drove] away.
- Mrs. Sawyer believes that Claudette's contempt for the man resulted in no further contact.
- Claudette had a string of two or three subsequent relationships that ended up on the rocks. The last one was with Mr. [DELETED] of Rochester, New Hampshire.
- Sometime in early 1988, Claudette needed a place to live for a while. Mrs. Sawyer said she was welcome to stay with them.
- There was no known contact with Anthony during that period.
- In February of 1989, Claudette left for Florida with her sister. She (they?) bought a house that their father owned in Delray Beach.
- During the last week of September 1989, she came up to New Hampshire to visit the Sawyers. She stayed until the first week of November. This, coincidentally, is the same week Anthony dropped out of sight in this area.
- During that period, she made approximately twenty-five phone calls, mostly long distance. Those are currently being investigated.
- The Sawyers promised to relay any further information to me.

At this time, we are following up on several leads in the New Hampshire, New York, and Massachusetts region. We have no recent reports of sightings in the Florida area so are prepared for the fact that Anthony may either be in a state of hiding in Florida or has moved on to another area. We believe that with an aggressive investigative effort he can be found. He has certain long-standing patterns that will tip his hand at some point in the future.

Phase Two

Investigations since the above initial report have proceeded as follows. On the night of December 18, I talked to Robert Jones on the telephone. He told me that he found a summons slip from the state of Maine issued to Anthony on September 19, 1989. It was apparently issued in Ogunquit. The summons slip stated the following information:

>Anthony Caruso
>[STREET ADDRESS]
>Glen Cove, New York
>[LOUISIANA DRIVER'S LICENSE #]
>[MASSACHUSETTS VEHICLE PLATE #]

Robert also stated that he was 99 percent sure that he saw Buddy in the same vehicle at his mother's house on October 13, 1989. The next day, I ran the plate number and it came back:

>Alamo Rent A Car
>[STREET ADDRESS]
>Ft. Lauderdale, Florida

I called Alamo in Florida and they referred me to the Boston office. I talked to D, the night manager. She was extremely helpful and cooperative. After two days of plate chasing, we found the car was a

>1989 white Buick Electra Park Avenue
>(just as Robert had reported earlier)
>[VEHICLE IDENTIFICATION NUMBER]
>[TITLE IDENTIFICATION NUMBER]

The car had been rented on September 18 by a Mr. Grover and returned to the Boston office on September 21. Due to the age of this transaction, I have not yet been able to ascertain more information on this individual. I am working on that currently. Then we checked usage on October 13, 1989.

According to Alamo, the car had been rented by a

>Dulio Bono
>Carbondale, Colorado
>[DATE OF BIRTH]
>[COLORADO DRIVER'S LICENSE #]

The car was reserved and secured with an American Express card. When the car was returned, the individual decided to pay the entire fee cash and put nothing on the credit card. D also told me that the individual said he was staying in a place called

[COMPANY NAME]
Swampscott, Massachusetts

I next called [SAME COMPANY NAME] and talked to M. He said that a Dulio Bono had indeed had reservations for October 12 through October 16, 1989. The reservations were secured with an American Express card: [CARD NUMBER AND EXPIRATION DATE]. The reservations had been booked on August 21, 1989, by

P.H. (initials only on this transaction)
Lynn, Massachusetts

M stated that the reservations were for three adults. But, nobody showed up for the room. The room charges were billed to American Express. A call to the fraud department of American Express, based in Arizona, connected me with Ms. S, regional investigator. Ms. S ran the card number and found that it indeed was registered to Dulio Bono and that the charges to Captain Jack's had been posted on the appropriate date. The card, however, had been reported stolen on November 1, 1989, and the charges were now considered fraudulent.

On Tuesday, December 19, I decided to call Mrs. Sawyer and see if she had had any contact with Claudette. She had not. I questioned her about any friends, etc., who might know anything. She said there was a friend of Claudette's, a girl named Irene who worked at BankEast who had gone down to visit Claudette just after Thanksgiving. Other than that she had nothing to report.

So, next day I went to BankEast. I found out that the girl was Irene Malone, branch director, whom I had known slightly for about eight years. I talked with her at length.

She stated that she had gone to Claudette's house the day after Thanksgiving and stayed for two weeks. They were together for virtually the whole time. Claudette was working as a temporary secretary so was gone some during the period. Irene went to one of the islands for two days, but other than that they traveled together most of the period. Irene even checked the answering machine frequently because she was expecting some calls. She states that there was ABSOLUTELY NO INDICATOR that Claudette had seen or had even been contacted by

Buddy. Irene states that Claudette was dating a couple of people she had known for quite some time.

With this new information, LS and I decided to go ahead and contact Claudette, feeling now that she was probably a friendly contact. I called and got her answering machine. I left a message requesting that she call me back. She did. The content of that call is as follows:

- Claudette informed me she met Anthony in 1973 in the dealership she was working at in Dover, New Hampshire.
- Most of the time she spent with Anthony she felt as if she were being held captive. In fact, he had threatened on numerous occasions that he would harm her children if she tried to leave him.
- She described Tony as a loner. He didn't spend much time in nightclubs.
- She also told me that he used aliases such as Bob Foster and also Anthony Coleman.
- She stated that he loved to impress everyone with gifts and entertaining in expensive restaurants.
- He had a very good memory, and used any information he obtained on anyone to his own advantage.
- The Shawmut in Kennebunkport was one of his favorite haunts.
- Tony had taken a trip with her to Vail, Colorado. They flew out; supposedly Tony had business there.
- He was apprehended and jailed in Eaglerock. He was charged with stealing a car in Massachusetts.
- Claudette flew back to Massachusetts to pick up her children at Tony's parents' house.

I called D from Alamo several times over the next few days. I asked her to run the names of some of Anthony's aliases. She came up with a phone reservation for Bob Hayes to reserve a car in September. There was, however, no follow-up and no charges posted. She also ran the name *Caruso* and came up with an interesting rental. On December 18, an Alamo rental office in Boston rented a Buick LeSabre [MASSACHUSETTS REGISTRATION NUMBER] to

        Joseph Caruso
        Lakewood, Colorado 80228
        [TELEPHONE NUMBER]
        [COLORADO DRIVER'S LICENSE #]
        [DATE OF BIRTH]

That rental had been secured with an American Express card. D said that this individual stated that he was staying at the Westin Hotel in Boston. She also stated that Joseph Caruso ended up paying very little ("around $9 if I recall") on the card because he used Delta frequent flyer coupons for the rental fee. Due to the Christmas weekend, I have not yet been able to follow up on Mr. Joseph Caruso fully.

On December 22, I called State Trooper Burgess of the investigative branch. She had been involved in the controlled-drug violation arrest of Anthony Caruso in September. She wants him [apprehended] badly. I asked her if she would run a Colorado check on both the Dulio Bono license number and that of Joseph Caruso. She said she would get back to me as soon as she got the information.

I called Ms. S [regional investigator for] American Express and asked her if the Joseph Caruso card was a stolen or abused card. She checked her file and stated that it was a valid card, used frequently, a lot of travel expenses. She also said that her files indicated that Joseph was working for a conservative conservation group and appeared on the surface to be legitimate.

That night (December 22) I called Robert Jones and asked him if any of the names were familiar. He said no. I asked him if there was any Colorado connection, and he said that his wife told him there was a cousin (possibly) in Colorado. Bob also told me that he had talked to Eileen (Buddy's ex-wife in Tampa). She told him that she was curious about one or more calls on her last month's phone bill. She said she didn't have them in front of her (her accountant had them) but there had been one or more calls made from Tampa area pay phones and charged to her business office number. She said that there was no reason for them and it was exactly what Buddy used to do. Bob told me she would get the information on the calls Tuesday after the Christmas holiday.

When I discussed the Joseph Caruso car rental, Bob stated that his mother had been acting much differently that week (still was). She would be gone from the house for several more hours at a time than usual. I decided to get up early the next morning (Saturday, December 23) and do a tail on Marguerite Caruso. LS and I picked the tail up at the [COMPANY NAME] at about 9:00 a.m. At about 10:45, she left the laundry and headed over to a small restaurant for some lunch. After approximately 45 minutes she left the cafe and headed over to 27th St. There, she picked up a small, white-haired elderly woman.

From there, we followed her to Revere, where she stopped at a small, Italian bakery. When she left the bakery, we lost the tail at a very congested five-way intersection due to traffic light timing. We tried to find her by checking all the local restaurants and the parking lots to all the hotels and motels. No luck.

I called Bob's home and got his wife. We decided that if she had another person with her, chances were almost nonexistent that she would be seeing her son. Bob's wife did say that an old place to meet was the Pewter Pot Restaurant on Route 60. We checked there with no luck. We returned home.

After a discussion, we decided to try calling Janice's father, Ray Clegg (mentioned earlier in the report). My talk with him soon revealed that he did know where Janice was. He said Frank Quato had contacted him. I explained the situation with Mr. Quato and that I understood the situation Janice was in. He softened up some and told me that Janice definitely was not with Buddy anymore, probably since about September. She was back with the father of her children and was trying to get her life back together. She just wanted to forget the whole thing and be left alone. He said she and he both wanted Buddy to be put away, but she was afraid of getting further involved. I asked that he pass the message on to Janice and that she give me some help. He said he would.

Christmas weekend saw no new progress. On Tuesday morning, December 26, I tried to call Trooper Burgess but she was out sick. I then called Brian Dennis to see if I could get some good pictures to send down to Claudette but he was not back from the Christmas vacation. My call to Mr. Brown did go through. I explained all that we were doing and assured him we would keep in touch.

Reviewing my notes, I was curious about the fact that back on October 13, we saw the possible fraudulent credit card charge on the card of Dulio Bono. Did Pam Howard (P.H. on transaction?) make the reservations back on August 21 and use the credit card number? If so, why was there such a long time gap between at least August 21 and November 1 when it was reported stolen?

I called Mark at Captain Jack's. He said that, indeed, Pam Howard had used that card number on August 21 to reserve the room. A call to Ms. S at American Express verified that. We were both curious about the time frame. She said she would give Bono a call and make some careful inquiries. In the meantime, I would try to see if that Colorado license number came back to the license of Dulio Bono or another person.

On Tuesday evening, I typed a letter to Janice. I will send this to her via her father and see if I can get a response. I am also attempting to contact the house detective at the Westin Hotel to see if there were any thoughts about Joseph Caruso.

On Wednesday, December 27, I decided to check further into the car rental information. I went back to the date of September 19, 1989, when a summons out of Ogunquit, Maine, had been issued to Anthony Caruso. As stated before, D at Alamo had stated that the car in question had been rented to one Artel Grover.

I asked the day manager, Ms. C, to check on this due to the question D had about the validity of the computer return. Come to find out that the car had actually been rented by one

James Graves
[STREET ADDRESS]
Tarrytown, New York

Mr. Graves had picked the car up from Boston on the night of the September 17, put approximately 580 miles on it, and returned it on September 20. Ms. C stated that the transaction seemed very "generic." There had been no credit card used to secure the transaction. Only $60 was placed down. This was in violation of company policy but not really that uncommon for commission-based rental agents. James Graves was required to give an employer and an employer telephone number. The agent was supposed to check these out before the vehicle was released. Mr. Graves gave the following:

[EMPLOYER NAME]
[EMPLOYER TELEPHONE NUMBER]

I asked Ms. C to fax the information to me, which she did. My first action was to check telephone information to see if there was such a listing. There was no person of that name on that street in Tarrytown, New York. Next, I dialed the number given for [STREET ADDRESS]. No answer. That evening, I ran all names connected with Anthony's possible patterns: James Graves, Dulio Bono, Joseph Caruso, Anthony Caruso, Buddy Caruso.

I also inquired about Anthony Caruso in National Crime Information Center (FBI) and found that he was now listed as wanted, originator Belknap Superior Court, extradition New England only at this time.

On Thursday, December 28, I called Alamo Rental in Boston. I asked if everyone would have been asked to show his driver's license at the time of rental. The clerk stated that they take the license and copy the license number off of it and onto the rental contract. That meant that either Mr. Dulio Bono himself had actually made the trip out here to Massachusetts or that, if this was Anthony, he would have had possession of both the credit card and license of Mr. Bono way back in August. If this were the case, why the time lag between reporting and loss/theft?

A PRIORITY TONIGHT WILL BE TO TRY AND DETERMINE IF MR. BONO HIMSELF HAD COME OUT HERE AND LOST HIS WALLET AFTER OCTOBER 13TH. [Note: Bounty Hunter's note-to-self is in all upper case for emphasis.]

Then, I called the New York telephone number given on the rental slip at Alamo on September 17. The call went through and a woman answered, "Mr. Gordon's office." I said, "I might have the wrong number." The woman immediately said, "You have the wrong number." I stated I was with a plumbing supply company. I then said, "This sounds like a legal office. I must have the wrong number." She said that it was indeed a lawyer's office. I thanked her and hung up.

I called Bob Jones and asked if the name Mr. Gordon meant anything. He said it had a familiar ring from way back and he would check with his wife. I looked through my file and found a note that Anthony may have used a truck from Florida to come up to New England in July. Bob said he thought it was a Budget Rental Truck. After many calls to Florida Budget Rental offices, I connected with Chris at the Truck Rental Division in Tampa Bay. I left him the information along with most of Anthony's aliases. He said he would get back to me.

Next, I called Mr. Harry Weitz at the security and fraud department for Visa and Master Card in Concord, New Hampshire. He was not in, so I left all the information with his assistant. She said she would give him the information first thing in the morning and he would probably contact me late morning.

My next call was to Tampa County Sheriff's Department—computer room. I had talked to these guys several weeks ago. I inquired about traffic violations linked to Anthony's aliases. I was told to call the Motor Vehicle Division in Tallahassee. No answer there.

Chase Manhattan Bank was my next move. I remembered Bob saying Anthony and his mother had accounts there. I talked to Mr. Carter at the downtown main office. He got back to me and said that there were no loans, savings accounts, or safe deposit boxes for Anthony or Marguerite Caruso. There was, however, a credit card for each of them. Anthony's had been opened July 1, 1979, and Marguerite's had been opened May 1, 1977. I would have to call the credit card department on Long Island for more precise information.

A call there revealed that both cards had seen little activity. In early September 1989, Mrs. Caruso had to pay $3,000 to clear up a heavily overused account. She had, however, left a balance of $83.80

that was now going into collection—due to its delinquency. I asked
what the last charge had been. It was a vehicle rental charge from the
Value Rent A Car agency in Tampa Bay, Florida, on July 14, 1989. The
vehicle charge was $1720.36 and had been made to Marguerite's card.

I called Value Rent A Car and eventually connected with Mr. S.
He said he had all the information on the transaction and that Marguerite had actually signed the rental contract herself. He asked that I fax
down a request for the information and he would fax it back up to me. I
did.

When I went to check the response to my fax request, I was denied the information because "he could not verify my connection with
the card holder." The information I requested would have to be given to
the card holder. Strange, since I had explained the whole situation to
Mr. S.

A discussion with Bob and Karen Jones Friday, December 29,
disclosed that there had been several phone calls made from the house
for which neither Bob nor his wife could account:

> Bethany, Oklahoma
> [TELEPHONE NUMBER]
> [DATE OF CALL]
>
> Tampa, Florida
> [TELEPHONE NUMBER]
> [DATE OF CALL]
>
> Tampa, Florida
> [TELEPHONE NUMBER]
> [DATE OF CALL]
>
> New York City
> [TELEPHONE NUMBER]
> [DATE OF CALL]

After thinking about it, Bob realized that the Tampa call made on
the 20th was to attorney Joe Episcopo. The others were unknown. I
would check them out Tuesday morning after the New Year's weekend.

They also told me that Marguerite Caruso had told them she was
going to her friend's house for the weekend and would not be back
until Monday night. They did not know where the friend lived. I told
Bob of the location we had tailed his mother-in-law to last week. He

said he would take a run by and check it out. In the meantime, Karen told me about several of Buddy's relatives and their recent actions.

The first was Buddy's second wife:

> Pat Kennedy
> Kingsport, Tennessee
> [TELEPHONE NUMBER]

There had been no contact for years until last year when she called just to "check and see how things were." Karen couldn't tell exactly what cover she could/would provide for Buddy if he contacted her. There was also a cousin in Colorado:

> Paul and Lillian (the cousin) Firestone
> Lafayette, Colorado

This Colorado link was interesting due to the credit card use of Dulio Bono, the Joseph Caruso subject, and now the cousin. Claudette had said that Buddy had taken her to Vail when they were together.

Bob called back later that night and told me that Marguerite's car was indeed at the #27 address over by the Old North School. But, he said that this was not the house of [THE FRIEND], whom she was supposed to be visiting. She, apparently, lived in the next town over, but nobody knew where. [THE FRIEND] had also let Marguerite use her car once when Buddy had come up to contact his mother. But, since we did not have any idea on the possible location, Bob would have to do some digging and get back to me. We would have to sit tight.

In the meantime, I contacted D at Alamo to see if any people/cars fitting the description had seen transactions. None. The other car companies were not online due to the time and holiday status.

The rest of the weekend saw no productive movement.

Tuesday morning saw the beginning of a hard push to track down movement patterns in the past months. First action was to contact the phone company and check on the numbers called from Bob and Karen's phone. Two will take a day or so.

The New York call was to:

> Lionel Bujold
> [JEWELRY STORE NAME]
> New York
> [TELEPHONE NUMBER]

I called Mr. Bujold. He was very cooperative. He reported:

- On October 25, a man walked into his jewelry store on 41st Street. He looked right at Mr. Bujold and said, "You remember me, don't you?" Mr. Bujold vaguely did.
- The man said he wanted to buy a watch and a ring. The watch was a cheap ($40) watch and the ring was a five-carat cubic zirconium valued at about $300.
- When Mr. Bujold asked about payment, the man emphasized again that he was familiar from the past.
- Also, he showed a "Social Security type" ID that Mr. Bujold had never seen the likes of before.
- He also told Mr. Bujold that he had a place in Glen Cove, New York, and a place in Pennsylvania.
- The man also wanted Mr. Bujold to make up an $800.60 ring but he refused to on an unknown check transaction. The ring was said to be for a customer.
- The purchase was made by check—name Marguerite Caruso.
- The check was bad and payment was not made.
- Mr. Bujold stated the man was about fifty, big, with white hair and a beard, dressed casually.

Karen Jones called and we talked for a few minutes. She told me a little about Buddy's son and daughter. They were actually his biological children. When Buddy broke up with their mother, they were both very young (the daughter may not have even been born). The son lives in Chelmsford and is about twenty-four now. I believe he lives with his wife or girlfriend. Karen believes that there has been little or probably no contact between them. The daughter is now about twenty-one and her name is:

Laurel Drew
[TELEPHONE NUMBER]

Karen states that about four years ago, Laurel came forward and stated she was being sexually molested by her stepfather. Apparently, her mother had to choose between believing her or her husband. She chose the husband and threw Laurel out of the house. As far as contact goes, Karen states that when Buddy got out of jail, he was looking for money. Karen overheard her mother talking to Buddy on the phone. Marguerite said, "Laurie doesn't have the money." Karen believes that Buddy may have contacted her. In addition, a couple of years ago Laurel went to Florida to reestablish contact with Buddy. Karen is unsure of the situation now, but thinks that Laurel is young enough to give in to a bit of pressure if it is applied right. Repeated calls to Mr. Dulio Bono have not yet made contact with him. I will continue to try.

Karen and I talked about Buddy's fascination with the Fire Service. We decided that it would be wise to contact the New York City Fire Service. I called the fire marshal in charge of investigations at:

New York Fire Department
[TELEPHONE NUMBER]

I talked for quite a while with them and left all the information. One inspector said he had just been talking to some officers that reported a big white male impersonating a fire officer. He would investigate and get back to me with any information.

I then called Discover Card headquarters and made contact with the security department. I talked to N at [TELEPHONE NUMBER]. We soon discovered that Marguerite did indeed have a card. Back in 1987, both she and Buddy were authorized users of the card number. But, later in 1987 she had his name removed from the card. Through 1988 and 1989 there was a tremendous amount of activity on the card. N stated there were somewhere around 235 postings and notations. Credit limit at that time was $2500. Then, in 1989 the card saw a flurry of activity that obviously got way out of hand. Many of the charges were for gas, motels, and other travel expenses up and down the East Coast throughout the summer. Charges got to be over $6000. Toward the end of summer the card was revoked by Discover and collection talks began. On October 4, 1989, Marguerite Caruso paid Discover a check for $6489 to cover past charges. I asked N what the last charges on the card were. She had two:

Budget Rent A Car, Orlando: $94.50, November 13, 1989
Budgetel Inn, Tampa: $512.18, October 23, 1989

These looked very promising. I first called Budget Rental and talked to S [TELEPHONE NUMBER]. She looked in the computers and could not find anything for that date. She only had a transaction for

Paul Caruso from Mansfield, Massachusetts, renting a car in Orlando and returning it to Tampa on December 2; Discover Card [CARD NUMBER]

I called N from Discover Card back. She stated that it looked as if the date she had given me for the rental was actually the date that the final payment for the rental had been posted. The car had actually been rented on June 23, 1989. The rental amount was $1,006. Apparently, because the card was so overdrawn it was charged back to Budget several times. When Marguerite finally made payment, the charge was posted in the computer. Thus, the November settlement posting looked like the rental date.

Next, I called Budgetel in Tampa. The clerk said I should call back in an hour. I did. I left the information with one of the owners. He said he would look it up and call me back.

In the meantime, I called the fire marshal's office in Tampa, Florida, [TELEPHONE NUMBER] and went through the same procedure as with the New York officials. They would post the notice and contact me about any activity.

N from Discover Card called me back to say she was still compiling information. She did tell me that Marguerite Caruso had just recently been issued a brand-new Discover Card that she might not even have received yet. There was only one card issued and the credit card limit was $1,000. I asked what we could do. She stated that Marguerite had full use of the card now. But N stated she would keep an eye on the activity of the card. As soon as the first purchase was made, she could cancel the card. That way, on the next purchase, the merchant would have to call in. If it were Marguerite, the purchase could be let through. If it were Buddy, they would call me right off. I thanked her.

When I returned, F from Budgetel had called. I returned her call. She had all the information. As with the Budget car, the actual stay had not been on October 23, but rather May 30 through June 11, 1989. Similar nonpayment and chargeback procedures had delayed posting on the computer until October. This is how the transaction took place:

- On May 30, a man walked into their inn.
- He said he wanted a room for one night.
- He gave F a Discover credit card to secure the room.
- The card was in the name of Marguerite Caruso.
- He asked, however, that she NOT charge the credit card.
- He would pay cash tomorrow when he left.
- He asked for a room for two, saying that his wife was with him.
- F never saw another person the whole time.
- Day to day, the man would say that he wanted to stay one more night and that he would pay cash tomorrow when he left.

- On June 10, he called the desk and told them that he wanted to stay just one more night and that he would be in in the morning to square everything away.
- He never showed up the next day and the inn was stuck with the charges for $512.18.

As she talked F remembered that when the man first came in, he asked if the inn had discounts. F said they did AARP. The man then gave his DOB as [DATE OF BIRTH]. The registration card he made out gave an address of:

[STREET ADDRESS]
Melrose, Massachusetts

F then stated that a short while later (a couple of days), she got a call from their corporate office. Corporate said that a man had called on June 11, and stated that his name was attorney Nathan Baldwin. This man stated that Anthony Caruso was a client of his and that he had left the inn and totally forgotten to sign the credit card slip when he left. He was extremely apologetic and assured corporate that a banker's check for the entire amount had already been put in the mail. Payment has never been received.

I asked F what the man looked like. She said she had no doubts about the man because of all the suspicions she had. The man was approximately 5' 9" tall, had very dark black hair, medium to dark skin, almost on the Mexican end of the scale, and weighed in the 175-pound range. I asked again if she were sure and she said, emphatically, yes.

On Wednesday, January 3, 1989, I tried to contact Mr. Bono again. I did get an answering service and she told me he would call me back shortly.

I then called several fire departments in areas that Tony might be in: Delray, Orlando, and Boca Raton.

I gave full information. Boca Raton stated that they would first call their police department and then us. I stated that would be fine.

Later that afternoon, I received a call from Mr. Dulio Bono in Colorado. I told him I was investigating some credit card thefts and asked if he would tell me what had happened. He said that in October, he had come out to Massachusetts for the wedding of a family member. He had rented a car and then stayed at a Holiday Inn over in (I think he stated) Melrose. He couldn't remember the car company and ran through a couple. When I asked if it could have been Alamo, he said it was. When I asked about lodging, he said now he thinks that he may have made reservations somewhere else but canceled them to stay at the Holiday Inn.

Then, after he got back, he was in a phone booth in Carbondale, Colorado. He is a contractor and spends time on the road, and also recently was thrown out of his condo when it was sold. He carried his wallet, etc., in a fanny pack. He set the fanny pack down, made his calls, then left. About a half hour later he realized he didn't have his pack. He drove back and found it was gone. But strangely, about a week later, the fanny pack showed up back at one of the jobs he was working on. I thanked him for his help.

I next made some calls and contacted the customer service center for Gulf Credit cards. Bob Jones said his mother-in-law had one. The operator informed me that she did indeed have a card, but that it had not seen any activity in quite a long time.

That night, I called Bob Jones to check on several things. He told me that he and his wife had been checking their phone bills from the past year and found several calls that they had not made:

February 21	###-####	
February 22	813 ###-####	
February 22	813 ###-####	Collect from Tampa
February 22	813 ###-####	Collect from Tampa
February 26	813 ###-####	Collect from Tampa
February 28	813 ###-####	Collect from Tampa
April 15	###-####	Plant City, Florida
April 18	405 ###-####	Bethany, Oklahoma
August 14	813 ###-####	
August 16	813 ###-####	Same #

On Thursday, January 4, I called the Royalton Hotel in New York to see if Anthony had stayed there recently. He had not. I then called Eileen Caruso to see if she had the mystery phone numbers from her accountant. She did, and unfortunately they were calls she had made and charged to her calling card. I next called Brian Dennis to check on the status of the picture of Anthony I needed and the paperwork I should have on hand in case I had to move fast. My next call was to Mr. Brown to keep him posted of our progress. No contact.

Friday, January 5, I went to the Dover Public Library and hit the phone books. First, I addressed envelopes for car dealers and fire departments/equipment suppliers throughout Florida. I stuffed them with flyers about Anthony and a copy of his most recent picture. Then, I called to find some information on Mr. Negin, the person I got when I called the number left by Buddy [*Caruso,* A POSSIBLE ALIAS WAS ON THE RENTAL SLIP] on the Alamo car rental slip. After a long search in Hubbel's Law Directory and the phone books, I found his address.

Making no real connection with any information to this point, I decided to call him. He was very helpful and cooperative, but had no idea who Buddy was or why he would use his name and address. He even offered any help if I needed some in the future.

Saturday was spent in Boston at Logan Airport. We hit all the car rental agencies and passed out flyers about Buddy. We even hit the area hotels and motels. The next several days we spent contacting fire departments and hotels/motels, passing out flyers.

Talks with Bob Jones indicated that his mother-in-law was acting quite strangely. She was out for hours during the day. Tuesday, January 9, she was not home at 11:00 p.m. when Bob called me. He and Karen were thinking that she must be with Buddy.

I got off the phone and made a call to Discover Card and asked them if she had made any purchases that day. They indicated that there had been a credit drop of $109 posted that day. But, they could not tell where it was from until morning.

I called Bob back and Karen answered. She whispered that her mother had just gotten back saying that she said, "Sometime you just owe it to yourself to play a while." I decided that I would come and sit on Marguerite the next day and see what happened.

Next morning, I got up and decided to make a call to Discover to see what the story was on the charges from yesterday. They told me that they had been made at Sears in Saugus. I left for Stoneham and got to the Dunkin' Donuts at about 8:45, an hour and fifteen minutes before Marge [Marguerite] gets off work. She was not there. I drove by her house and she was not there. Strange, but nothing could be done about it at this time.

I decided to go to Reading Fire Department and see Bob. He was out on a call. I decided to go to Sears in Saugus. Karen had said that her mother showed up with a new pair of sneakers yesterday, so I went to the shoe department. Nobody recognized a picture of Buddy or remembered Marge from the day before. I went up to bookkeeping, but they could not determine what department she had been in or sort out what she might have purchased.

I decided that, on the outside chance Buddy was in the area, I would hit all the motels/hotels/inns I could in the area. I traveled all the way down through Burlington, leaving flyers with Buddy's picture.

When I returned to Reading, I talked to Bob. He stated that they had had a call early in the morning. At about 7:00 a.m. they had gone by the Dunkin' Donuts and Marge's car was there. On the way back, at about 7:30 a.m., it was gone. Bob and I discussed the possibilities. Was Buddy in the area? Had Marge skipped with him? Bob explained that January 12 was the day that he had to let Marge know what he wanted to do about the house: either not exercise his exclusion option, which would mean that Marge would sell the house and he and the family would have to find quarters; or, he would decide to stay in. If he chose to stay, he said he would only do it if Marge would sell the house to him and Karen for one dollar, then he could get a mortgage for about $90,000 and pay everyone off.

If Marge refused, which was the obvious thing to [expect would] happen especially if Buddy was counseling her, he would go off the wall with Marge. Perhaps this would force her to see, or call Buddy and make a slip.

I returned to Bob's house and sat in observation. At about 5:00 p.m., Marge returned alone and went into the house. That evening was quiet.

I returned to the fire station to talk with Bob. He told me that Karen reported Marge stating she had been sick and left work early this morning to come home and rest. At about 10:00 p.m., Karen called and said she overheard her mother on the phone with a friend. She said she was not going into work next morning. But then Marge asked Karen's son to check the alarm clock to make sure it was set for 4:00 a.m.

I decided to sit on the house all night. I also called LS and told her she might want to come down in case we had to run a two-car tail. She did. We sat on the house all night. No activity. LS returned to Dover at about 9:00 a.m.

At about 11:00 a.m., Bob met me around the corner. He was almost at a loss for words. He said he had just confronted Marge with the request that she sell him the house for a dollar and she had quietly stated that that was fine with her. She told Bob to take care of the arrangements. She indicated that she did not want to see Bob and the kids without a home and she just wanted to resolve all the problems this situation had created.

Bob also said she said things like she wished Buddy were in custody so the $50,000 would be freed and that she was all through with Buddy financially. Bob left for some errands, and I sat on the house. Marge went out about noon, but just went to the store and returned home. No more activity until she was picked up at about 6:30 p.m. to go bowling. I returned to Dover.

Next morning, Bob and I talked on the phone. Marge had gone to work as usual. When she came home, she had called the real estate agent and taken the house off the market. This was a very strange turn of events. What had happened and when? I told Bob that now might be the time to start emphasizing the family ties on this end and impressing on her that if Buddy were in custody, there would be $50,000 free for all to use. An apartment could be built for Marge so she could stay in her own familiar house. He agreed to pursue this avenue.

There was also a sighting of Buddy and Marge in Norway, Maine, on the second weekend in November. This was the latest sighting yet. We would follow up on it this weekend.

Sunday, LS and I went to Norway, Maine. *Way* up in the boon-docks—a very unlikely spot for Buddy. We hit the police and fire departments and all local motels and restaurants.

That night, a very strange thing happened. LS got a call from a person who identified himself as Brian Nelson. He asked if a guy by the name of [UNKNOWN NAME] were there. LS asked who he was (that was supposed to be there). Brian said that he was a friend. Brian had wanted to get in touch with him, so he called his parents who lived in Orlando, Florida. They had said that [SAME UNKNOWN NAME] was visiting up here in New Hampshire and was staying with LS at [LS's ADDRESS AND TELEPHONE NUMBER]. He said perhaps they had read the wrong number out of their book. He also said he was from the other side of the family. Brian said he lived at [STREET AD-DRESS] in Dover, New Hampshire.

He stated he would call back in half an hour to see if his friend had called. LS and I tried to figure out what was going on. The only people we could make a connection with were the Clegg family, who had received the letter from me. About forty-five minutes later, he had not called (as we suspected). We called the number, and it was a mobile phone with no occupant at the time. Was it one of the people from LS's work who may suspect our part in a drug bust the night before?

The following night, LS and I went to the [Nelson] address. There was a male and a female in the house. We asked them about the call. They stated that they had no knowledge of the call or the names. We both felt that they were not telling the truth. We would pursue the matter further in the future if warranted.

For the next several weeks, we were at an impasse. I sent out approximately three hundred more flyers to police and fire departments and car rental agencies throughout the Northeast and the West. I also spent several weekends sitting on Marguerite Caruso. No remarkable movement or actions. Bob Jones continued to proceed on the paper-work for transfer of the house and securing bank financing.

During the third week of January, Bob called and said that a friend of his mother-in-law's had seen a motel key in Marguerite's purse. All she saw was that it was from the Blue Roof Motel. I checked most of the New England phone books and came up with the Blue Roof Motel in Kittery, Maine. I went over and talked to the night manager. He was very helpful. He did not remember the picture, but allowed me to look at the registration books for October through January. No luck on the name. I felt that he would probably use a name like Graves or Hayes, so I copied all such names and dates. I said I would return.

The next week saw more surveillance and flyers. No breaks.

Then, on February 4 at 10:00 a.m. during the blizzard, I was beeped on my pager by the manager of Days Inn in Burlington, Massachusetts. He stated that the subject on our wanted poster had just left their facility in a white van. I called Bob Jones and told him to get down there as fast as possible. He arrived about ten minutes after Buddy had left. Bob went out trying to locate the van. We arrived about forty-five minutes later. We talked to [MANAGER'S NAME] and his desk assistant. They described the events like this:

- On Saturday, February 3, about 6-9 p.m., a man came to the desk and identified himself as R. Clinton.
- He stated that he was an IBM executive and wanted Super Saver rates. He said he made reservations but the desk clerk was unable to find them. That never happens.
- They gave him a room and the low rates—$63.75 for one night and a $10 key deposit.
- They had [ROOM NUMBER].
- He was not using a credit card, so the desk required cash and a license. He said his wallet was in the car. He came back, took money out of a woman's wallet, and showed his "wife's" license:

    Dolores Clinton
    [NEW HAMPSHIRE DRIVER'S LICENSE #]

- The address he gave was:

    [STREET ADDRESS]
    Kittery, Maine

- In the morning, he came to the desk to check out. He said that he had to go check on a flight.
- At about 2:00 p.m. he showed up again saying that he could not get a flight out and needed a room for one more night—at low rates.
- The desk clerk stated that she was not sure she could offer the low rates again. She went out back to the office to check with [MANAGER'S NAME].
- Then, Buddy started in on "Don't you know who I am? I really work for Days Inn and you are all in big trouble. First you lose my reservations and now this!"
- At this point he stormed out of the lobby saying he was going to the Marriott.
- Through the back window, the clerk thought they might have left in a white van that was just pulling out of the parking lot. At about this time, they realized that he was the man on the wanted poster.

Our talk with the staff revealed he had been wearing mirrored sunglasses, a red flannel shirt, and a light brown parka. We went through the trash in the room and found:

> two large containers of Chinese food remains
> petite panty hose box
> parking ticket stub from Somerville
> partial receipts from Jordan Marsh and Ames
> muffin box from Publix at Sturbridge
> note referring to coats
> fruit package from De Moulas

We left the Days Inn and spent five hours hitting every motel and hotel within a ten-mile radius, to no avail. Before we left the area, we stopped in to see Bob and Karen. Karen said that every item in the trash reflected her brother's habits.

From there, we traveled to Kittery to check out the Bridge Street address. Nothing—as expected. [Next we went to] the Kittery police—not familiar. I also found out when they tried to run Buddy in [criminal database], he didn't come up. The birth date was wrong.

[Then we went] to every motel and hotel in the area. No luck.

Next day, I ran the license number and got an address [IN HAMPTON, NEW HAMPSHIRE]. I checked the building out. There were no people at home at the time.

A trip back to the Blue Roof Motel [the key that had been seen in Marguerite's purse] yielded the fact that Buddy had registered as James Williams [one of the frequently used aliases] on September 15. He put down the vehicle license as [MASSACHUSETTS LICENSE PLATE NUMBER], which meant his mother was with him.

Over the next several days, I ran complete credit checks, vehicle checks, and reference checks on Dolores Clinton. Nothing!

Several nights of sitting on the house came up with nothing. Running of a plate in the yard came up with a Lorraine X who worked in Hampton at [COMPANY NAME]. This was apparently Dolores's roommate.

After weighing all the options on who might spook and whose side who was on, I decided to call the building owners, Raymond and Sandra Randal. A young man answered and stated that his parents were on a cruise in Florida or something. I said I was a friend of Dolores from way back. He said she had moved out or something about a month ago.

I now knew that [Lorraine] should be approached. We made several attempts to make contact over the next couple of days. We finally made contact on Sunday evening, February 18, approximately 8 p.m. The next three hours proved remarkable.

- [ADDRESS AND WORK DELETED] Lorraine was the tenant of title for the Randal house.
- Dolores Clinton had moved in with her approximately one year ago as a roommate. They had not been friends before that time.
- Somewhere around the first part of November, Dolores met Buddy Caruso, who identified himself as Paul Williams from New York, at a Parents Without Partners meeting in Portsmouth [NEW HAMPSHIRE].
- Lorraine described Dolores as a woman desperate to find a man and live in that fantasy world. She had nearly gotten married the previous year on a whirlwind romance and had been married three times before.
- The "romance" with "Paul" progressed mainly over the phone with occasional dates. Dolores is heavily into tarot cards and wrote many notes about the "good" signs for her and "Paul."
- As Christmas approached, Dolores invited her whole family up from all over, including her daughter, Dawn, from Virginia.
- Lorraine bought all the food and made all the preparations.

- The whole family showed up on Christmas morning. "Paul" showed up early and he and Dolores left, leaving Lorraine with a house full of strangers.
- "Paul" and Dolores [sometimes called Dee] returned about noon. Dinner and much bullshit [sic] about how he was a millionaire filled the afternoon. Lorraine was already suspicious.
- Buddy and Dee left again about 6 p.m., leaving Lorraine again with a house full of strangers.
- Buddy and Dee popped in and out over the next several days. They supposedly went to New York sometime between Christmas and New Year's Day.
- Lorraine left for a previously scheduled Florida trip on December 28. The house [was left] full of strangers.
- When Lorraine returned from vacation, she received a hefty phone bill for $300 and was left without a roommate. Dee had taken off with Buddy and left all her belongings there. Calls to Dee's family and friends brought no satisfaction.
- Lorraine learned that Buddy's mother, Marguerite, had come up to her house for New Year's Eve.
- She also learned that Buddy and Dee had split and taken Dee's daughter, Dawn's, credit card.
- Dee's brother, Ron, who was a cosigner on the loan for the van Dee used for business, had also come up to repossess the van due to [Dee's] failure to make payments.
- On February 5 or 6, Lorraine received a note from Dee postmarked from New York City. [It was a] brief card saying she was having a wonderful time with "Paul."
- Dee's daughter, Dawn, tried to make contact with some of the hotels that were on her calling card bill. Buddy and Dee were charging telephone calls to one of Dawn's cards. Several of the calls were to MW, a very good friend of Buddy's mother. [When Dawn called her] MW played dumb, asking, "Who? What does he look like? Where is he from? How would I know him?" MW had been used as an intermediary in the past between Buddy and his mother.
- Lorraine also called Buddy's mother to tell her to have Dee give her a call.
- Lorraine has a friend in a nearby police department to whom she gave the license plate number on the black Mercedes Buddy was driving. It was a New York plate.
- The officer had run it and come up with the plate registered to an Ahamed Hassan.

- Lorraine had also looked into several of the numbers on her phone bill. Three of interest were:

Russell Gansen	401 [NUMBER]
Frank Franco	401 [NUMBER]
Danvers Trust	508 [NUMBER]

- Lorraine mentioned that Dee and Buddy had gone skiing in the Plymouth/North Conway/Loon areas and mentioned looking for a house to buy.
- Lorraine was financially strapped and wanted to get a new roommate to help pay for the rent and utilities. Could she sell Dee's belongings? I advised her to contact her lawyer. She placed an ad in the newspaper to the effect that the belongings would be sold and also posted a registered letter to Dee's post box in Seabrook.
- A surprising finding was that Dee was *very* deeply involved in astrology and tarot readings. A fascination with crystals was also evident. She also had a collection of explicit adult magazines.
- Lorraine was somewhat fearful for her safety and worried about Buddy breaking into the house to retrieve Dee's belongings. I told her to call me if anything suspicious happened. She agreed to do anything necessary to help.

As we left Hampton, I stopped at the police department and explained the whole situation. Hampton police said they would keep an eye on the house and area.

Several days later, I contacted Ron Clinton (Dee's brother) who operated [BUSINESS NAME] in Plaistow, New Hampshire. I spoke with him on the phone and made an appointment with him to meet for a talk (he was cautious over the phone). Our meeting revealed that he was a very concerned and "friendly" contact.

Dee had worked as a talented designer for him over the past years. When she met Buddy, she became a different person. Ron indicated that his sister was looking for a fairy tale after several recent bad experiences with men. She had blinders on and was only seeing what she wanted to see. As much as he cautioned her about Buddy, she saw what she wanted to. Ron was very concerned that Dee had burned a customer in Long Island for about $600 and had for all intents and purposes completely neglected her accounts and responsibilities.

Since her disappearance with Buddy, she had no direct contact and he feared for her safety. Ron agreed to do anything he could to assist the investigation.

My next contact was with Rick, Dee's son. He lives in Seabrook and works for [COMPANY NAME] in Amesbury, Massachusetts. Rick indicated that he was formerly employed as a credit investigator and would also do anything possible to get his mom back. Rick said that he was a co–key holder of his mother's post office box and that he would meet me at the post office that Saturday morning to check the box.

I met him. There was a great deal of mail, including the letter from Lorraine. The box had obviously not been checked for weeks. We spent a great deal of time viewing the mail and discussing the whos and wheres. Rick and I left agreeing to keep in close contact and share pertinent information.

February 20 came and went and the [bond for Anthony] forfeiture date passed. Bob Jones had to pay the $50,000 fee. A long discussion indicated that if we could still produce Buddy, there was a good chance that the state of New Hampshire could be petitioned to return a percentage of the forfeiture money due to the extreme financial strain it put on the Jones family.

I agreed to continue the hunt, even though we had received *no* money to this date and the possibility of payment in the future was questionable.

LS and I were scheduled to leave for a vacation in Florida to last from March 6 until March 30. During the last week of February, Rick contacted me and said he had received a postcard from his mother from New Orleans. An interesting card he had also received indicated that she and Paul (Buddy) had gotten married and they were enjoying a wonderful traveling honeymoon.

The day before we left for Florida, we received another call saying that they were in New Orleans. When we arrived in New Orleans for the start of our vacation, we spent several days checking hotels, motels, and clubs. No solid evidence. We did find one hotel [employee] in the French Quarter [who] felt Buddy had stayed there the night before. The registration card was made out by a Richard Graves from Tallahassee, Florida.

As we progressed up across Florida, we checked out many locations associated with Dee's family or Buddy's past history. In St. Petersburg, we tried to contact Dee's parents, but they were out of town. The rest of the vacation saw no other serious progress.

When we returned from vacation, I called Rick. He said that he had received several cards from his mother from various locations around the country. Several days later, he called to tell me that he had received a package from his mother. It contained souvenirs from places like New Orleans, Cape Kennedy, Disney World. A note said that she and "Paul" were having a wonderful time and that they would be back in the area in a short while. She looked forward to seeing the family.

During this entire time I was sending hundreds of wanted posters to police departments, fire departments, hotels, and motels up and down the East Coast.

[There were] several more cards from Dee to Rick. A package came from San Francisco with souvenirs from the West. There were also several videotapes from a store in San Francisco. Rick had called the store, and they basically said that the tapes had been stolen.

Then, around the first part of May, a major event happened. Rick called me and said that he had received a package from his mom. The package had come into his possession in the following way:

- In their travels, Dee and Buddy had apparently stopped in Tennessee and sent a package, addressed to themselves, to the following address:

        [STREET ADDRESS]
        Asheville, North Carolina

- They continued on their travels.
- UPS attempted to deliver but couldn't due to insufficient address information.
- UPS looked up the return address and saw that Dee had used her post office box in Seabrook, New Hampshire (*the fatal mistake*).
- UPS then sent a letter to that address requesting advisement on shipping. Rick got the letter, called UPS, and asked that the package be shipped to him.
- It was.
- He got it and inventoried it. Inside were:

    a license plate [MAINE LICENSE PLATE NUMBER]
    several appliance instruction manuals
    a couple of sweaters
    various souvenirs
    quote from a printer in Asheville for business cards and invitations
    a mini videocassette

I asked Rick for the person who had sent him the letter from UPS and the reference number. It was as follows:

C. M.
[PACKAGE ID NUMBER] 42 lbs.
[COMPANY NAME] Printing
Asheville, North Carolina
[TELEPHONE NUMBER]
Owner: M.G.S.

I called and reached Ms. S. She was hesitant to talk over the phone. I asked if she would feel more comfortable if I faxed down a copy of my IDs and credentials. She said yes and I did. We then talked at great length. She stated that the quote was for business cards Dee wanted for a miniatures company she wanted to start. The quote was made March 13, 1990.

Ms. S said she remembered the incident vividly. Dee went on and on about the wonderful, extremely rich man she had just landed. They were moving into the area. They had seen a house they liked and were now trying to bypass the real estate agent to sweeten the deal. They had been traveling extensively and now were off to Colorado. Dee said her husband, Paul, was across the street having their Mercedes looked at in the Midas Muffler shop. Ms. S said she saw the black Mercedes across the street. Dee finally left. Three days later, Ms. S saw the Mercedes and Paul across the street. I asked Ms. S for the phone number of the Midas shop and a realtor in the area. I thanked her and told her to contact me if they returned or called.

My call to the Midas shop proved typical. Buddy had walked into the shop and started yelling at the clerk saying that he had had his muffler fixed in the Midas shop in San Diego. The job had failed and he demanded it be fixed by them at once at no charge. A work order had been made up and the muffler fixed.

When I asked what information was on the work order, it was found that the only slip missing for the whole year was that one. Buddy had apparently taken both copies of the slip. The shop owner stated that he had called the San Diego shop, and they said that he had pulled a similar scam out there.

My next call was to [COMPANY NAME] Real Estate in Asheville, North Carolina. I explained the basic situation and asked if they were familiar with Buddy and Dee. They stated no. They gave me the numbers of many real estate brokers in the area. I called most of them. No luck.

Rick called again. We talked about the progress I was making. He then told me that there was also a mini videocassette in the box. It was of Buddy and Dee at various places. I immediately told him I wanted a copy on VHS. He said he would have to have a copy made and get it to me. LS picked it up two days later.

The video had the best images I had ever seen of Buddy. It showed him and Dee in Washington during February. It then showed them in the hills of Tennessee. There were then shots of a residential valley shot from the back porch of a house. Their base? There was a strange structure on a distant hillside that we would try to identify. The last shot was of Dee in the car saying that they were in Maggie Valley. I called out to the Maggie Valley Chamber of Commerce and inquired about the couple and the car. No immediate luck, but they would call as they uncovered information.

Another call from Rick. He received a card from his mother stating that they would be back in the area very soon. The return address was [STREET ADDRESS], New York, New York.

A search of listed and unlisted numbers in New York City could only come up with a

P.A. Graves
[STREET ADDRESS]
New York City
[TELEPHONE NUMBER]

As with most addresses in the past, my assumption was that this one was fictitious and a compilation of historic remnants.

For about a week and a half I sat and waited. Then, on June 8th my beeper went off. It was CM. She stated that a man had just walked into the UPS terminal in Asheville (I thought she said) and inquired about the package. Fortunately, the clerk was familiar with the situation. The clerk, wanting to buy time, said that the package was not there but in Atlanta in the main terminal.

The clerk also told Buddy to call MG [UPS loss prevention manager]. Buddy asked who he was and why he should call and was told that he handled all lost packages and it was just standard procedure. Buddy stated that he did not want the package shipped up to Asheville because they were going to be in the Atlanta region the first of the week so they would pick it up. He also said he would call around 3:00 p.m. to verify pickup location.

At this point, I felt that if Buddy had walked into the Asheville office and was not planning on leaving for Atlanta for several days, I should go to Asheville to try and pick him up that weekend.

Travel arrangements were initiated. But a subsequent discussion with UPS showed that Buddy had not walked into the Asheville office, but had actually walked into the Nashville office. That made immediate travel south illogical.

I then spent hours on the phone with MG and the loss prevention people. I was now directed to the Atlanta UPS loss prevention manager, DC.

- I had to start almost from scratch with the Atlanta UPS people.
- I had to fax down all pertinent information.
- Verification of *wanted* status proved interesting.
- The problem of "extradite New England States only" would prove sticky.
- UPS also was nervous about a "nonpolice" operation.

I knew that Buddy would walk into the terminal at his own time. I knew I had to set up the process so that when Buddy walked in, which I knew could be in a day or three weeks, he could be scooped immediately. This made 911 response the only feasible response.

My calls then became directed to DeKalb County sheriff's department. This required a key individual who would be completely familiar with the operation and be able to see that it came to fruition once it started. I found a very positive resource in one, Lt. Ivy, DeKalb County Sheriff's Department.

Through long discussions with him and the faxing of all pertinent information, response to a 911 call from UPS was assured.

Discussions with Brian Dennis the week before had concluded that Bob Jones should call a New Hampshire attorney to negotiate with Ed Fitzgerald (Belknap County Attorney) for guarantee of hold and extradition status with Georgia and North Carolina. That was done.

Many phone calls to both UPS and the sheriff's department made me quite confident that the trap was set. Now, we waited.

Buddy had stated that he would be in Atlanta the first part of the week of June 11. I felt that he would not follow that predictable schedule. We waited that entire week.

The weekend of June 16–18 was spent doing a fugitive recovery from Massachusetts. Then, Tuesday morning my beeper went off. It was Lt. Ivy stating that Buddy was at the UPS terminal in Fulton

County. It was not his jurisdiction and he was acting as an intermediary. He stated that Fulton County needed verification from New Hampshire that they did, indeed, want Buddy.

A desperate call to the county attorney's office got an official to call Lt. Ivy with verification. He passed this on to Fulton officers. Buddy put up a fight and tried to bully his way out of the arrest. But the wanted poster with vehicle information, a picture of him, and physical description confirmed identity.

After more than half a year the arrest was made!

Epilogue to Case

At that point, I felt quite at ease that only administrative details remained. We would go to Atlanta, pick him up, and return him to New Hampshire.

I even called Florida authorities at the Tampa sheriff's department to check on his warrant status there. He did indeed have a number of active felony warrants against him.

I explained that I would like to look into the way in which we might bring him to Florida when New Hampshire was done with him. We would even pay the freight if need be just to get him off the street. The officer said he would pull the file and forward it to the state's attorney's office in the morning. He thought that it would fly.

One more call to Fulton indicated that Buddy would go for a preliminary hearing at 8:00 a.m. on Wednesday. I would call early to make sure that all holds were in place and that nothing might go wrong.

Next morning I called a Lt. Proctor with the Fulton County Sheriff's Department, who indicated that there was a bit of trouble with extradition status in New Hampshire. Another call to Ed Fitzgerald's office and the Belknap County Sheriff's Department and a request that they call Fulton County again appeared to answer any existing questions. I was told to await a call from Belknap County Sheriff's Department as to when we could come and pick Buddy up. I waited.

About 2:00 p.m., I received a call from one of my employees who stated that DC from Belknap County had called and said they were going to release Buddy because Fulton County could not hold him.

Another desperate call to Belknap verified that.

Fulton County said that they could not release Buddy to anyone but a law enforcement agency. My deal with the state had been that they would guarantee hold and extradition and that we would personally pay the freight for getting Buddy back here.

I asked if we could get temporary deputization status (I am a New Hampshire police officer). No way.

Could we pay the fare for one of their deputies to go with me to pick him up? No.

Could we hire one of the numerous off-duty deputies to fly down with us? Can't spare the manpower.

Could we get a sheriff from another county? Can't be done.

Can you think of any way that will work for you? After all, I have eight solid months of free time in on this guy and he deserves to be taken off the street and put in jail. No.

I was not about to let New Hampshire politics let this reprehensible person walk out the back door. So, I turned to Florida again. I called the state's attorney, Tampa, Florida.

He was hurrying out the door but gave me a minute. He was familiar with the situation after my call the night before initiated the inquiry. He briefly looked at the file and said that they normally only extradite for first-degree offenses. But since Buddy had so many charges and was just in Georgia, he leaned toward extradition. He had to run but would get back to me shortly with a decision.

About a half hour later, Officer BD from Tampa called me to discuss the matter. He said that they found a couple more unresolved charges against Buddy and that they definitely wanted him. He would immediately call Lt. Proctor in Fulton County and verify the Florida hold and extradition.

My heart and pancreas returned to a more normal level of operation.

A subsequent call with Lt. Proctor confirmed that the hold had indeed been put on.

How do you spell *relief*?

[I made] several more calls that night to Fulton to verify that all holds were in place. The records people at the jail said Buddy was scheduled to end his time served with them on Saturday or Sunday. There were nine pages worth of paperwork in his files in reference to the hold from Florida. There was no question as to his extradition status.

A call from R. Clinton and his family came in about 3:00 p.m. They stated that a man posing as a lawyer from New York had called in reference to Dee's planned bankruptcy filing. He said she did not want to involve the family and a check would be cut in a day or two to pay them what was owed. He just needed Dee's phone number to work out some details.

Rick had gone to Atlanta Tuesday evening to pick his mother up and drive her back. When Buddy was arrested, she had $3,800 cash on her. There also were no holds or warrants on the car. Therefore, Atlanta released her with both the money and the car.

At about 9:00 p.m. on Thursday, I received another call from Rick. He was at his sister's house in Newport, Rhode Island, with his mother. She was saying that she had no idea of what was going down and that she would testify against Buddy if needed. But, Rick also said that Buddy had called and stated that he was getting out Sunday and would see her soon.

I explained what the actual situation was and they all felt relieved. About 11:00 p.m., I got a call from Bob Jones. He was not happy with the apparent games that New Hampshire was playing over the extradition. It appeared that New Hampshire was trying to avoid possibly having to pay back the $50,000 or any part of it.

I urged Bob to call his lawyer and Brian Dennis in the morning and try to see if there was anything that could be done to get him up here to New Hampshire on Friday.

Friday morning had my first call from BD, Tampa Sheriff's Department. He stated that all was set on the extradition. I asked what Buddy might be looking at, and he stated that the charges represented serious jail time. In fact, four of the charges were not bailable. I explained that Buddy had jumped bail both here and in Florida to the tune of $65,000 during 1989. We told each other we would keep in close touch as the situation developed and new warrants were issued.

My final call was to Brian Dennis at 2:07 p.m. on Friday. He stated that Bob Jones had not called. We talked. It was concluded that it was obvious that Buddy would not be coming to New Hampshire for the weekend. He would be extradited to Florida, and whatever administrative deals we planned would have to be worked out later through Florida.

I had done all I could do to this point without legal help from a sharp criminal lawyer, and that would have to come from Bob's end. Until further notice, the case of Anthony Caruso lies at rest.

Components of the Thick Description

The lengthy description of a single bond-skipping case given above is a thick description of an information-seeking episode. It might be asked: "Why is such detail necessary?" The crux of a reply would be that it is only with such thick description that we see the importance of small details, the importance of persistence, the importance of personal commitment, and the importance of analyzing failures for clues to new paths. Of course, thick description carries with it its thickness; it is easy to lose one's way in the details. There follow tables that distill the points of the story.

Table 4.1. Content Analysis of Activities

Analyzing
 Strange telephone call

Arresting
 Fugitive

Calling
 Bail bond company (6 times)
 Building owner
 Car rental agencies (various—8 times)
 County sheriff
 Credit card companies (9 times)
 Ex-wife of fugitive
 Father of woman involved
 Fire marshal
 Fire services (numerous)
 Hotel
 Karen
 Midas (2 times—fugitive seen)
 Motel (3 times—confirm use of stolen card; fugitive seen)
 New York City Fire Service
 New York jeweler (3 times)
 Owner of stolen wallet
 Possible contact (3 times)
 Relative of fugitive
 Robert (11 times)
 Sawyers

Son of fugitive's wife (7 times)
Source (3 times)
State trooper (2 times)
Supposed employer
Tampa sheriff
Telephone company information
Telephone number on rental slip
UPS security (4 times)

Checking
Address
Credit card use (2 times)
Fugitive's aliases
License plate numbers (numerous)
National criminal database

Contacting
Bail bond agency
Brother of fugitive's wife
Building owner
Car rental manager
Fire and police departments (numerous)
Florida bail bond agency
Son of fugitive's wife (2 times)
Telephone company
UPS security

Discussing (with)
Bail bond agency (2 times)
Sheriff's department

Distributing
Flyers (wanted notices—while vacationing in Florida)

Evaluating
Evidence
Situation

Faxing
Police (arrest arrangements)
UPS

Following
>   Fugitive's mother
>   Fugitive's relative

Inquiring
>   Police department
>   Post office

Locating
>   Possible girlfriend

Mailing (note also *sending*)
>   Flyers (wanted notices—2 times)

Meeting
>   Robert (3 times)

Observing
>   Coast
>   Fugitive's mother (2 times)
>   House (2 times)

Reviewing
>   Notes

Running
>   Credit card checks (numerous)
>   License plate number
>   Vehicle

Sending (note also *mailing*)
>   Flyers (wanted notices)

Talking
>   Bail bond agency
>   Contact
>   Karen (2 times)
>   Possible lead
>   Robert (4 times)
>   Sawyers
>   Trooper
>   UPS security

Using
    Public library

Visiting
    Address in strange call
    All motels in 10-mile radius
    Bob and Karen
    Burlington (wanted notices)
    Logan Airport (wanted notices)
    Norway, Maine (wanted notices)
    Police departments
    Relative
    Robert
    Sears (interview staff)

Simple model of process, especially if taken as a known-item search:

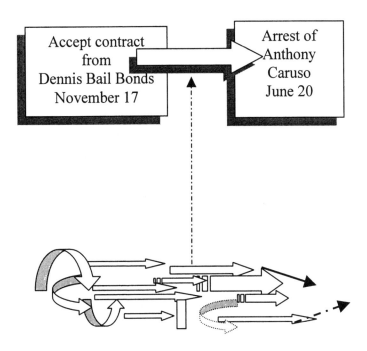

Figure 4.1. Bounty Hunter Search Components

This model reflects the variety of tactics, number of collaborations, and constant juggling and evaluation represented in the case study and in conversations with the bounty hunter.

Table 4.2. Fifty-Two Stories to an Arrest

1. Claudette Pellerin
2. Robert Jones
3. Marguerite Caruso
4. Mr. & Mrs. Sawyer
5. Janice
6. Royalton Hotel, New York
7. Eileen Caruso
8. Pepe Clark
9. Frank Quato
10. Alamo Car Rental, Florida
    - Sept. 18 Artel Grover
    - Oct. 13 Dulio Bono
11. Irene Malone
12. Trooper Burgess
13. American Express
14. R. Clegg (Janice's father)
15. James Graves (alias?)
16. Mr. Gordon
17. Budget Rental in Florida
18. MVD, Tallahassee
19. Chase Manhattan Bank
20. Value Car Rental, Florida
21. Pat Kennedy (second wife)
22. P&L Firestone (cousins)
23. L. Bujold (NY jeweler)
24. Laurel Drew (daughter)
25. New York Fire Dept.
26. Discover Card
27. Budget Car Rental, Florida
28. Budgetel Inn in Florida
29. Fire marshal in Tampa
30. Fire departments
31. Lawyer—Negin (car rental)
32. Picture & flyer campaign
    - Library
    - Fire departments
    - Airport
    - Car rentals & dealers
    - Hotels
33. Sears
34. Brian Nelson
35. Clegg family
36. Days Inn manager
    - Event description
    - Suspect description
37. Examine trash
38. Kittery Police
    - License number
39. Blue Roof Motel
40. "Who might spook?"
41. Lorraine's story
42. Roy's story
43. Dolores Clinton
44. Dawn (Dee's daughter)
45. Dee's brother, Ron
46. Dee's son, Rick
47. UPS
    - Self-addressed box
48. Discount Express Printing
49. Midas
50. RE/MAX
51. Maggie Valley Chamber of Commerce
52. Plans with UPS and local law enforcement

Table 4.3. UPS Thread: The Fatal Mistake

1. First steps: make contact with Claudette P. and Robert J.
2. After a long phone conversation, appointment with Robert J.
3. During first meeting with Robert J. learn:
    *   Anthony Caruso has habit of using false/stolen credit cards
    *   Anthony Caruso has Visa and Discover Card
4. Call to Discover Card
    *   Marge has a Discover Card
    *   Marge and Anthony Caruso both have use
5. Caruso of Massachusetts rents Budget Car in Orlando
    *   Card seriously overdrawn
    *   Last purchase made on Discover Card
6. Continued checking from Natalie at Discover Card
7. Marge was issued a brand-new Discover Card
8. Discover—Sears charge in Saugus, Massachusetts, on new card
9. Distribution of posters in several northeastern states
10. Call from Days Inn, Burlington, Massachusetts, re: guy in poster
    *   Used Dee's ID to book room
11. Contact made with Ron (Dee's brother)
12. Contact made with Rick (Dee's son)
13. UPS package to self
    *   Return address
    *   To Dee's son, Rick

Some Thoughts on Bounty Hunting

At first, a bounty hunt gives the appearance of a known-item search. After all, the name, the Social Security number, and other attributes of the fugitive are known. However, in a known-item search the known attributes map directly to a known location. This does not necessarily mean that the search is trivial; that known location of a book might be several floors away or in remote storage. It is also possible that the book will be misshelved or checked out. It is also the case that some bounty hunts can be like known-item searches. There may be an address at which the fugitive is actually residing or there may be a recent sighting. The bounty hunter then needs only to go to the location and, with some caution, make the arrest.

Generally, known-item searches depend on the stable, diachronic attributes of the document. This is the sort of attribute one finds on a wanted poster. The fugitive's name, height, weight, scars, etc., are listed. A typical case brief or story demonstrates that functional, dynamic, synchronic attributes are the more useful elements in an actual hunt. For the bounty hunter the question is not "What is the fugitive's name?"; rather it is "What do I need to know in order to end up where the target is?" That is, what attributes of the fugitive's character and situation can be elicited to predict a location. Again, the crucial, indeed the target, attribute is the functional attribute "where." Unlike the case of the book, the diachronic attributes of the fugitive do not map to location, and the fugitive is likely to attempt to obscure and confuse the issue of address. UPS turns out to be the terminal story, however was in no way predictable from the original given diachronic attributes of name, height, weight, last known address.

Bounty hunting, also termed *fugitive recovery*, can be thought of as an information profession. Note that some threads attempt to find data, others attempt to establish patterns, still others attempt to generate new leads. The general pattern of activity is to

- generate several threads or lines of investigation
- establish, monitor, maintain, generate collaborators
- monitor all the lines of investigation
- evaluate progress
- generate new threads
- modify threads
- abandon threads
- look for anomalies
- inform the generation and monitoring of the threads with previous experience and knowledge of what fugitives do.

In discussing the mind-set of statisticians who use exploratory data analysis (EDA), Gluck characterizes their activity with comments that fit the bounty hunter model by quoting Hartwig and Dearing:

> Statisticians conducting EDA are more concerned with retaining a lead that may turn out to be useful later; that is, they do not wish to reject prematurely a hypothesis that later may turn out to be useful. They are exploring and tolerate dead ends and false starts with the optimism that the exploration of some possibilities will lead to important results subsequently that premature rejection would have precluded. (Hartwig and Dearing, 1980, cited in Gluck 2000, p. 696)

Chapter 5

Frameworks for an Emerging Image of Engineering Design

Jud Copeland

We turn here to a different form of case story. We distill the story of engineering design work from the writings of several explorers of the epistemological foundations of the field. Humans as engineers, engineering as intrinsically human might well be another way of talking of hunting and gathering. Both are ways of speaking of direct engagement with significant problems. Here we use a combined method of distillation and content analysis of works on engineering. Distillation requires an iterative process of paring down the writings to only those portions dealing with the topic at hand; content analysis here looks at the frequencies of word occurrence across several authors.

Few authors examine design activity as a human problem-solving process. In an inductive theory-oriented study of such a topic, Creswell (1994) states, "substantial literature orientation at the outset" may be required to "frame" and "counterframe" the topic under investigation (p. 24). Distillation allows a conceptual framework or "map of the territory being investigated" (Miles and Huberman, 1984, p. 33) to evolve inductively. From a holistic perspective, distillations represent the "rich context" (Creswell, 1994, p. 21) from which an image of engineering design will emerge. Krippendorff (personal communication, April 7, 1997) states that the distillations can serve as an inferential framework that informs the data about engineering design as a human problem-solving activity. They are the "thick description" (Rudestam and Newton, 1992, p. 39) for generating inferences about the data (key words) and categories of design activity. Figure 5.1 models the approach to using existing literature for framing, counterframing, and generating inferences about engineering design activity as a human information-seeking activity.

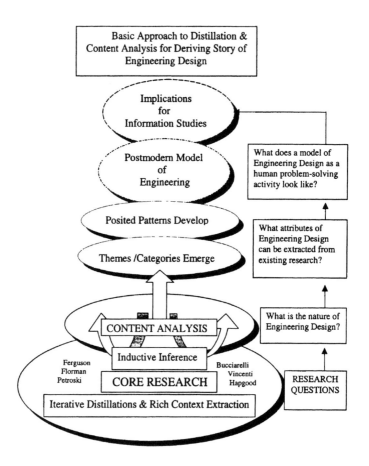

Figure 5.1. Model of Approach to Analysis of Engineering Design, Adapted from Copeland

A content analysis of core research frames using an inductive or inferential mode of inquiry allows themes and categories of design activity to emerge. The themes in turn stimulate "substantive theories" (Merriam, 1988, p. 86) about engineering design. These theories imply "conjecture and speculation" about the nature of design activity; they are "an imaginative formulation of underlying principles" (*Principia Cybernetica,* 1997) of engineering design.

Patrick Wilson (personal communication, January 28, 1997) posits thoughts on the nature of models that extend the above definitions. He asserts:

> The term "model" is very loosely used, especially by social scientists and it can be applied to any deliberately over-simplified representation of a situation or process, whether given in mathematical terms or verbal description, plus or minus diagrams or other visualizations.

Wilson's description of a model provides a framework for exploring other research that addresses issues surrounding the development of a model of engineering design.

One other element of the epistemological environment within which we are examining engineering design warrants consideration here. The distinctions between modernist positivist modes of reasoning and those of a postmodernist approach play a significant, almost counterintuitive role. Chia's (1995) ideas on the "different styles of thinking" in research analysis can illuminate salient points about the nature of models. In particular, his thoughts on modernist and postmodernist thought styles are useful as an interpretive framework for examining issues surrounding a model of engineering design. Figure 5.2 identifies and contrasts the characteristics of this postmodern model with one derived from modernist assumptions. Rorty (1991) asserts that modern and postmodern modes of thought can be distinguished by their "epistemological priorities." These are best understood as differences in styles of thinking, each with their own set of ontological commitments, intellectual priorities, and theoretical preoccupations.

According to Chia (1995), a model based on Nagel's (1979) notion of a scientific theory being based on an abstract calculus and operational definitions represents a modernist thought style. It relies on a strong ontology of "being," a distal state that privileges thinking in terms of discrete phenomenal states, static attributes, and sequential events. It models a linear style of thinking in which things and entities rather than relations are privileged, and it implies that one can control, predict, and generalize research outcomes of any given phenomena (Chia, pp. 579-581).

Placing the MODEL at the top of the postmodern portion and surrounding it with a permeable border speaks to the emphasis on a useful solution that may or may not continue to hold beyond the present use. The MODEL is supported from, part of, and not necessarily the pinnacle of a set of multiple threads. The threads are shown as numerous, not necessarily direct, and not necessarily complete (dotted lines); yet capable of supporting the MODEL at multiple points. We do not mean to imply that modernist approaches have no utility; only that focusing on the method in an exclusionary fashion eliminates possible approaches to problem solution.

Whitehead (1985) asserts that this thought style accentuates a view of social reality as comprising discrete, static, and hence describable phenomena; it is a deductive mode of thinking that "turns verbs into nouns, process into structure and relationships into things" (p. 69). The modernist style sees physical objects and things as the natural units of analysis ("givens") rather than, more properly, the relationships between them. Whitehead calls this tendency the "Fallacy of Misplaced Concreteness" (p. 69). The "paradox only arises because we have mistaken our abstractions for concrete realities" (Whitehead, p. 69). Models based on a strong ontology of being tend to conceal alternative models or styles of thinking. An engineering design model based on postmodern thinking privileges a weak ontology of "becoming" which emphasizes dissonance, disparity, plurality, change, and even ambiguity, paradox, and the "not-yet-known." It views the phenomenon of design activity as "a processual, heterogeneous and emergent configuration" (Chia, 1995, p. 579). The postmodern sensibility is a proximal style of thought in which design activities are deemed to be continuously in flux and transformation and hence unrepresentable in any static sense. It is an inductive and analogical mode of thinking that uses a verbal approach to describe "emergent relational interactions and patternings" (pp. 581-582) that underlie the dynamics of design.

In a broader sense, a postmodern thought style is an attempt to "de-center" modernist thinking about the nature of engineering design. It enables one to think about ignorance and uncertainty in the "respectable" terms cited by Smithson (1993). As such, it becomes an exploration of the negative spaces of engineering in a human context, and an attempt to think, as Davidson (1978) notes, in metaphorical "visions, thoughts, and feelings" rather than in "concrete articulations" of modernist literalism (p. 41). The "gap to be bridged here is not one of slight attitudinal differences, but of differing perceptions" about engineering design, of alternative ways of thinking about "the processual actions and movements" (Schwartz and Ogilvy, 1979, p. 24) of design activity.

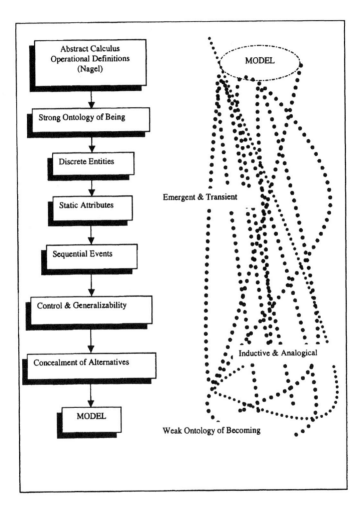

Figure 5.2. Modernist and Postmodernist Research Assumptions. Concepts Adapted from Chia; Figure Adapted from Copeland

Chia (1995) asserts that adopting a postmodern mode of thinking in research implies radical consequences for theory and model development in any given field. A model of engineering design based on a postmodern thought style is a response to Chia's assertion. It is a postmodern "counterframing" of design activity. In particular, it is a response to Blair's (1990) argument for an alternative way of thinking about the nature of one's engagement with research and to Laudan's (1984) "apologia" for an alternative model of engineering design. Further, it is an opportunity for stimulating a dialectic approach in research on design activity, and it is a dynamic framework for engaging Harris's (1986) "extended argument" in the field.

What might the emergent categories reveal about engineering design as a human problem-solving activity? There are no formal guidelines for discussing the results of an inductive, qualitative research design. Yet Creswell (1994) as well as Rudestam and Newton (1992) suggest a direction that is useful for discussing the implications of findings on design activity. It is an opportunity for the researcher to "move beyond the data and to integrate creatively" (Rudestam and Newton, 1992, p. 121) the salient themes on engineering design. It is largely an exercise in inductive thinking, grappling with discovery, meaning, and understanding in the rich "context bound" (Creswell, 1994, p. 5) data of design activity. It is an exploratory "treasure hunt" (Rudestam and Newton, 1992, p. 124) that seeks to make sense of the emerging categories of engineering design.

The researcher allows the data and implications "to be judged on their own merits and not on [his] amplification of them" (Rudestam and Newton, 1992, p. 124). The reader will discover that the data infer impressions of design activity as a human problem-solving process. In a broad sense, the findings are "conceptually informative" and address problematic issues identified in Information Science. In particular, they are a response to the gap in the "ongoing dialogue" (Marshall and Rossman, 1989, p. 89) in the field of engineering design. As substantive theory on design activity, the data or categories of engineering design can be inductively linked to a "larger explanation" or "grand theory" (Merriam, 1988, p. 94) for an "interpretive, artistic, [and] systematic" (Smith, 1987, p. 66) treatment of the phenomenon, and "for developing a story or patterns from detailed categories or themes" (Creswell, 1994, p. 44) of design activity. The categories and themes imply "broader conceptual and theoretical statements" (Rudestam and Newton, 1992, p. 123) for model development in the field of engineering design.

To stimulate discussion of the findings of this inquiry, the reader may ask: "So what" (Rudestam and Newton, 1992, p. 12) for engineering design? If the researcher allows the data "to speak for themselves" (Weber, 1990, p. 62), what do they imply about design activity? The categories derived from content analysis of the distillations make "explicit certain entities" (Marr, 1982, p. 20) or salient themes of design activity by each author. Specifically, each author reveals categories or themes that suggest a "tentative conceptual framework" (Creswell, 1994, p. 97) for engineering design. What "explicit entities" does each author contribute to an emerging "pattern of interconnected thoughts [for] making sense" (Neuman, 1991, p. 38) of design activity? What contextual themes infer "thick description" (Rudestam and Newton, 1992, p. 39) for a substantive theory of engineering design?

Ferguson (1992) perceives engineering design as a highly visual, artistic, and nonverbal process involving pragmatic and contingent themes. One sees an intuitive and sensual image of design activity. Human error and failure in design activity are placed in a rich context of intuitive, visceral, and even "messy" activities. The process is further characterized by whimsical, erratic, and unpredictable patterns of behavior. Ferguson suggests that engineers often reach tentative solutions to problems; this involves a relational fit between solution and problem characterized by a leavening effect in design activity.

For Petroski (1985, 1989), human failure (or error) is a dominant theme in a pragmatic, iterative, and subjective context involving the engineer's imagination. The engineer engages in an emerging discovery process that often leads to satisficing solutions to problems. It is a design context characterized by sloppy and somewhat fuzzy categories of activity. The themes of design activity are highlighted by tacit and implicit qualities that are elusive in nature to the engineer who experiences them.

Hapgood (1993) describes engineering design as a metaphorical traversal through solution space in which explicit themes of human failure, imagination, and stuckness surround design activities. It is an idiographic and unpredictable experience that often involves a painful series of trials or iterations in solution space. The engineer is perceived as a tinkerer who engages in activities within an artistic and subjective context.

According to Florman (1994), the salient themes of design activity are tacit; they are often difficult for the engineer to articulate. Design context is an introspective, artistic activity that is fundamentally pragmatic and contingent. Florman reveals it as a human process shaped by evolving existential patterns within an inductive and intuitive framework. This subjective process is highlighted by evolving themes of uncertainty, failure, and error.

Bucciarelli (1994) interprets design activity as a contingent problem-solving process characterized by a high salience or degree of uncertainty. The engineer as bricoleur uses scenario-building techniques in an evolving context of ambiguity. Human failure and error come into play as the engineer searches for a pragmatic, satisficing solution to problems. This is an idiographic experience, a metaphorical process pushed by imagination, an iterative technique forming a bricolage as a tentative solution.

From Vincenti's (1990) perspective, engineering design is a highly conceptual and intuitive human technique shaped by contingent and pragmatic categories of activity that are tacit and nonverbal in nature. The engineer often engages blindly in a design context, adaptively using imagination, failure, and error in a mental winnowing process to achieve satisficing solutions to problems. Vincenti suggests that engineering design is sometimes an overtly messy, fumbling activity.

Each author contributes "meaning" and "understanding" (Creswell, 1994, p. 145) to an emerging image of design activity. Yet these salient themes provide a "fragmented framing" (Entman, 1993, p. 51) or "contingent" perspective (Creswell, 1994, p. 22) of engineering design. Integration or "re-contextualization" of the salient frames (or dominant categories) "results in a higher level of analysis [by providing] a larger, more consolidated picture" (Tesch, 1990, p. 97) of this phenomenon. It reveals an emerging, holistic image of design activity as a human problem-solving process that is explicitly pragmatic, contingent, and visual in character. The integrated themes imply that the design engineer's engagement in solution space is a highly introspective and conceptual activity stimulated by instances of failure, error, and uncertainty. In a metaphorical sense, the engineer acts simultaneously as artist and bricoleur to discover satisficing solutions to problems. A salient pattern of "whimsical" activity suggests an underlying sense of humor in engineering design.

These attributes of engineering design—satisficing, messy, holistic, whimsical, nonverbal, and embracing failure—are from the studied writings. The results of key word extraction are presented in tables 5.1 and 5.2. The first presents total usage of terms across the six studied authors; the second presents the number of authors using the most frequently occurring terms.

Table 5.1. Engineering Key Words

Combined key words extracted from the rich distillations of the writings of Ferguson, Petroski, Hapgood, Florman, Bucciarelli, and Vincenti. Note that the terms are ordered in ascending order of number of uses, rather than alphabetically.

Terms	Uses	Authors	Terms	Uses	Authors
elusive	2	1	fitness	6	2
emerging	2	1	idiographic	6	2
fumbling	2	1	inarticulate	6	1
fuzziness	2	1	tacit	7	2
leavening	2	1	blindness	8	1
puzzle solving	2	1	sensual	8	1
sloppy	2	1	evolving	9	3
tinkering	2	1	metaphorical	9	2
discover	3	1	iterative	11	3
exploratory	3	1	uncertainty	11	2
painful	3	1	satisficing	13	3
tentative	3	1	solution space	16	1
adaptive	4	1	subjective	17	4
bricolage	4	1	introspective	18	1
implicit	4	1	imagination	22	4
inductive	4	1	error	23	5
scenarios	4	1	nonverbal	23	2
stuckness	4	1	conceptual	24	1
traversal	4	1	intuitive	25	3
trial	4	1	artistic	28	3
unpredictable	4	1	visual	28	1
visceral	4	1	contingent	32	4
messy	5	2	pragmatic	37	5
winnowing	5	1	human	41	6
ambiguity	6	1	failure	48	6
existential	6	1			

Table 5.2. Extracted Key Words Ranked by Number of Authors Using Each Word

Terms	Authors
failure	6
human	6
error	5
pragmatic	5
contingent	4
imagination	4
subjective	4
artistic	3
evolving	3
intuitive	3
iterative	3
satisficing	3
fitness	2
idiographic	2
messy	2
metaphorical	2
nonverbal	2
tacit	2
uncertainty	2

Key words present one distilled sense of the epistemological foundations and human characterization of engineering design. We can enrich this sense with fragments from each of the author distillations:

Ferguson

- Most of an engineer's deep understanding is by nature nonverbal, the kind of intuitive knowledge that experts accumulate.
- [M]aking wrong choices is part of the same game as making right choices.
- [I]nformal negotiations, discussions, laughter, gossip, and banter among members of the group will often have a leavening effect on the outcome.
- The mind's eye is the locus of "remembered reality and imagined contrivance." Collecting and interpreting much more than the information that enters through the optical eyes, the mind's eye is the organ in which a lifetime of sensory information—visual, tactile, muscular, visceral, aural, olfactory, and gustatory—is stored, interconnected, and interrelated.
- [M]essy nonscientific decisions, subtle judgments, and human error...

Petroski

- Engineering is a human endeavor and, thus, is subject to error. Failure considerations and proactive failure analysis are essential for achieving success.
- We are all engineers of sorts, for we all have the principles of machines and structures in our bones.
- When failure does occur, it becomes critical that engineers perform a "postmortem expose."
- [T]he solution reached in any given engineering design is not necessarily an optimal one.

Florman

- It's time for technologists—especially engineers—to stop letting themselves be pigeon-holed as soulless dullards and [to] joyously proclaim their identity as "craftsmen": builders and makers, heirs to all human ambition and curiosity.
- [E]ngineers are members of a profession that has its roots in the earliest development of the human species.
- [On "existential"] ...its most essential meaning: (1) the rejection of dogma, particularly scientific dogma; and (2) reliance on the passions, impulses, urges, and intuitions that are the basic ground of human existence.
- [E]ngineering is a basic instinct in humans that emerges naturally from our genetic constitution. Man's abilities to mold, to carve, to build and also to devise are evolutionary developments, adaptations in problem solution derived from the Darwinian theory of natural selection.

Bucciarelli

- [C]onsensus about the thing that becomes, is the product of social negotiation among engineers....Technology as it is is irreducibly historically and socially contingent, the product of muddling through and hassling about.
- Ambiguity and uncertainty are especially evident at the interfaces where participants from different object worlds must meet, agree, and harmonize their design proposals and concerns. Ambiguity allows room to maneuver, to reshape, to relearn and come together again. It serves as an ephemeral connection between bricolage and "do-it-yourself" in engineering design.
- [H]uman aspect of concept formation in the design process through the image of a human heart, embodying the pragmatic and contingent nature of engineering design while allowing for elements of ambiguity, paradox, and uncertainty.

Hapgood

- Obviously, he thought, there was a way; he must be an idiot. He began to experience a sense of the idiographic or emic nature of engineering as a human activity....Blanco's exhaustion had released him from his over-attachment to his prior experience with other problems and forced him to refocus his attention on his experience with the [current] problem.
- The process is an iterative one that embodies pattern generation and recognition. Decision and systems theorists sometimes refer to these volumes of plausible answers as "solution spaces" and to problem-solving as defining paths through these volumes, as "searching" solution space.
- What humans do is...think up a completely wrong but sincerely intended approach to the problem, jump in, fail, and then do an autopsy. Each failure contains encrypted...directions to the next step in the process.

Vincenti

- [E]very technology is a completely human construct.
- [O]rganizing the design is the core process by which engineering knowledge is generated....The process typically involves tentative layouts of the arrangement and dimensions of the artifice, testing the candidate device or solution to see if it does the required job, and modification of the candidate solution when it does not. The design procedure is complex and usually requires several iterations.
- Engineering knowledge reflects the fact that design does not take place for its own sake and in isolation. Artifactual design is a social activity directed at a practical set of goals intended to serve human beings in some direct way.

The integrated themes are the "vehicle that [inductively] communicates" (Miles and Huberman, 1984, p. 24) an emerging, substantive theory of design activity to the researcher. Yet how does one move from "substantive theory" or "thick description" of engineering design to a "larger explanation" or "grand theory" (Merriam, 1988, p. 94) for interpreting this human phenomenon? What "interpretive, artistic" grand theory can the researcher use to create a visual model inferred by substantive theory of design activity? How does one "systematically" model a "context bound" substantive theory of engineering design?

Blair (1990) cites two possible alternatives for developing a model of design. The researcher could adopt Nagel's (1979) scientific theory as an interpretive, systematic "grand theory" (Merriam, 1988, p. 94) and use its "abstract calculus" and "operational principles" (Nagel, 1979, p. 83) to develop a model of design activity. This scientifically assumptive formula would compel the researcher to develop a list of attributes that define a normal scientific model (such as Nagel's) and then use them to systematically interpret design activity. The researcher could cite those scientific qualities or categories that engineering design lacks, then propose means to remedy the lack of fit between engineering activity and the scientific model. In other words, the researcher could "upgrade" the themes of engineering design so that they match the attributes of an objective, rational scientific model.

We might ask: Why does Blair even consider a scientific "stance" for interpreting data on engineering design? Why must one feel compelled to scientifically "legitimize" the categories of design activity? Blair questions the fundamental nature of Information Retrieval from a scientific perspective and wonders if the field is a "legitimate science" (1990, p. 277). Perhaps Blair feels compelled to respond to the "compulsive force" (Fleck, 1979, p. 39) of a "prevailing" positivist epistemology in the field (Harris, 1986, p. 529). Even Machlup and Mansfield (1983) note the "guilt feelings" and "inferiority complex" researchers experience when their research designs do not garner the "honorific designation" of "hard" science (p. 13).

Does this sequential, linear approach fit the assumptions of an inductive, qualitative study of design activity? Does it respond to the impressions of engineering design as a human problem-solving activity? What entities of design activity are illuminated or made explicit (or indeed, overlooked) by this technique? Does it allow for "artistic" interpretation of the phenomenon?

Shortland (1981) challenges Nagel's scientific assumptions and asserts that his theory is "ambiguous, confused and lacks precision" for application to any given field of study, not to mention engineering design. He further asserts that "the trouble with Nagel is not so much with what he examines as in the serious things he has left unexamined" (p. 475). For Shortland, the "greatest danger" lies in Nagel's assumptions about use of scientific theory as a basis for generating models in the social sciences. He cautions against adopting "arbitrary and incoherent" approaches "that imply a strong, positivist orientation in their line of inquiry" (Shortland, pp. 476-477).

Blair (1990) agrees that Nagel's "straightforward" theory may serve as "symbolic generalizations or operational definitions' (p. 279) for developing models in natural sciences, but finds it inappropriate for inductively generating a model of design activity. Nagel's theory is a powerful "thought style" that "predetermines what researchers think they see" (p. 282) by exerting a "compulsive force upon their thinking" (Fleck, 1979, p. 39). It unconsciously frames the way researchers interpret the phenomenon of engineering design by deluding them "into thinking that they see pure facts in a reality unadulterated by preconceptions" (Blair, 1990, p. 281). Nagel assumes that facts are objective and context-free. According to Blair, they are not. Facts or data are "intimately connected to an endless number of other facts" and they achieve degrees of "salience" or distinction only within the context of a model that emphasizes some aspects of a given phenomenon over others (Blair, pp. 281-282).

Kahneman and Tversky (1984) further suggest the implications of using scientific theories or frames to generate a model of engineering design. Framing as a technique selects and illuminates some feature of reality while omitting others. In other words, while frames may call attention to particular aspects of the phenomenon of design activity, they simultaneously, and logically, direct attention away from other aspects. Most frames are defined by what they omit as well as by what they include; the omissions of potential problem definitions, interpretations, and solutions may be as critical as the inclusions in guiding the researcher. In addition, Edelman (1993) notes the character of any given phenomenon becomes "radically different as changes are made in what is prominently displayed, what is repressed and especially in how observations are classified" (p. 232). From this perspective, engineering design can be viewed as a "kaleidoscope of potential realities, any of which can be readily evoked by altering the ways in which observations are framed and categorized" (Edelman, p. 232).

Weber (1990) asserts that a traditional, positivist approach such as Nagel's often "overlooks or misses" data derived from inductive use of content analysis (p. 52). In addition, it "tends to destroy semantic coherence ... making interpretation extremely difficult, if not impossible" in qualitative designs (p. 43). The "rich" substantive theory that implies a model of engineering design in a human context "may not surface" (Creswell, 1994, p. 7) or find an opportunity for expression in Nagel's scientific definition for models.

Ferguson (1992) argues that Nagel's scientific "formula" attempts to frame engineering design as a formal, sequential process that is deductive in nature. Design activity is defined as a step-by-step process (diagram) of discrete, linear segments that, if followed according to Nagel's prescribed rules, leads to predictable outcomes. For Ferguson, this static approach inevitably leads to other "block diagrams" of engineering design. Specifically, it overlooks or misses salient themes (and categories) of design activity that emerge from inductive content analysis of engineering distillations.

Blair's (1990) argument for a model of engineering design grounded (embedded) in "perspicuous examples" of design activity does not fit the positivist assumptions of Nagel's scientific formula. The "growing undercurrent of urgency" (Blair, p. viii) for new, alternative models of engineering design becomes "unthinkable and unimaginable" in a strong positivist "thought style" (Fleck, 1979, p. 39). Thus, Blair remains a "Pickwickian prisoner" (Popper, 1970, p. 56), caught in the framework of the "older language" and unable to break out of it to propose a new, more appropriate model or metaphor for translating design activity. In a similar vein, Laudan's (1984) "apologia" for more appropriate theoretical models in engineering design cannot be "translated with validity" (Weber, 1990, p. 78) into Nagel's straightforward definition. For Laudan, model building remains "embryonic" and "locked inside an impenetrable black box" of technology (p. 1).

In a broader sense, Harris's (1986) use of "extended argument" to stimulate models for problem solving in Information Science finds no dialectical expression in Nagel's scientific framework. There is no opportunity to generate alternative models to challenge the "prevailing" positivist epistemology in the field. Thus, the "dialectic of defeat" is sustained through "scientistic delusion" and "ludicrous misapplication" of positivist technique (Harris, 1986, pp. 515, 529).

Guba and Lincoln (1985) and Creswell (1994) caution researchers concerning "lack of fit" between purpose, approach, and theory in qualitative designs. According to the authors, the "lack of fit" becomes clearly evident when "findings and implications seem to make no apparent sense in light of the original questions" (Guba and Lincoln, 1985, p. 226). A scientific interpretation of themes of design activity makes "no apparent sense" in light of engineering design as a human problem-solving process. In addition, a scientific technique, such as Nagel's, is not appropriate for inductively developing an emerging model of engineering design based on "thick descriptions" of engineering distillations. Engineering has been "barking up the wrong metaphor" by attempting to adopt a scientific model of design activity.

Blair (1990) suggests an alternative approach for developing a potential model of engineering design. It is based on the "perspicuous examples" in which design activity is embedded. His notion of perspicuous examples fits the assumptions of themes inductively derived from "thick description" or "context bound" substantive theory of engineering design. Sniderman, Brody, and Tetlock (1991) would characterize Blair's thoughts on design activity as a "potential counterframing" of the topic (p. 52). The authors argue that a rigid, scientific model constrains and inhibits any attempts at counterframing engineering design. Similarly, Machlup and Mansfield (1983) assert that "indoctrination with an outmoded philosophy of science, with persuasive (propagandist) definitions of science and scientific method" is a "mischievous" (p. 13) practice that precludes development of creative counterframing techniques.

Yet counterframing can provide the researcher with alternative ways of thinking about design activity and, perhaps more important, they stimulate alternative perspectives for viewing problem definition, interpretation, and solution within the rich context of engineering design. For Fleck (1979), these alternative modes of thinking are the "counterframes" that challenge a thought collective's normative assumptions on design activity. They are a potential source for generating alternative "pathways of thought" that can extend beyond the "perceptual dissonance" and "intrinsic constraint" of a "dominant metaphorical thought style" (pp. 158-160).

How does the researcher advance a "potential" counterframing of design activity that will enable him to be "more spontaneous and flexible" in exploring an emerging model of this human phenomenon? How can he elaborate a "countervailing trend" that "calls for sidestepping the artificiality and narrowness" (Rudestam and Newton, 1992, pp. 29, 32) of Nagel's scientific formula? Slater (1967) offers an initial response to this question. He cites the need to develop theory and models in the social sciences from an inductive, qualitative stance. He exhorts researchers to begin this effort by "picking over the detritus and shards" of data overlooked by scientific methods. Slater hints at a rather "eclectic conceptual montage" for generating models "derived from neglected avenues of exploration" (p. 101).

Smith's (1987) reference to an "interpretive, artistic, [and] systematic" (p. 66) treatment of human phenomena suggests a viable path for counterframing engineering design. It is an inductive, exploratory approach that involves taking "risks inherent in an ambiguous procedure"; it allows the "biases, values, and judgment of the researcher" to come into play (Creswell, 1994, pp. 4-5, 10). Yet it is this subjective mode of inquiry that stimulates "nondirectional thinking" about a potential counterframing model of design activity. Specifically, it focuses on elaboration of a "systematic" schema or model of design activity and then extends to "artistic interpretation" of engineering design themes within the context of this tentative conceptual framework.

Generating a Model

In taking the role of a counterframing researcher, I inductively generated tentative models of design activity simultaneously with data col-

lection and analysis. This "reflexive" technique involves the "specula-
tions, feelings, problems, ideas, hunches, impressions, and prejudices"
of the researcher (Bogdan and Biklen, 1992, p. 121). Further, it is a
"trial-and-error" process in which the researcher moved between the
themes or "substantive theory" of engineering design and a "grand theory" (Guba and Lincoln, 1985, p. 245) for interpreting an emerging
model of the phenomenon.

What are the architectural impressions of an emerging model of
design activity? Are there conceptual blueprints that can provide a
"glimpse" of this evolving configuration? Mintzberg, Bohm, and Black
advance ideas for systematically shaping a model of design activity. In
particular, Mintzberg (1994) asserts that researchers who attempt to
model human problem-solving activity often emphasize only one salient aspect of the phenomenon. "Heeding the advice of any one of these
researchers" must of necessity lead to a "lopsided" perspective on problem solving as a human activity. Mintzberg stresses it is critical to
"show all components" of a model in a single integrated diagram. Only
in this way can scholars understand the "richness" of this human phenomenon. In addition, it reminds scholars "at a glance" that the various
components that make up a model of human activity cannot be "conceptually separated" (pp. 21-22).

Mintzberg advances thoughts on constructing a model:

> I think there is something to the fact that the model pre-
> ceded the text. What matters in developing theory about
> human activity, in my opinion, is not so much the fully ar-
> ticulated text as the comprehensive representation of the
> model. People need to "see" the various dimensions that
> appear to constitute the phenomenon all in one place. That
> way, they can begin to discuss human activity comprehen-
> sively and interactively. I found this to be true as I started
> to use the model to develop the theory, and when I drew the
> diagram on a napkin at dinner one evening. (1995, p. 363)

Mintzberg's (1995) model emerged within an informal context
and preceded any textual articulation of underlying theory. The current
model of design activity emerged from dominant themes of engineering
design before a textual narrative or interpretive script was developed.
That is, the systematic structuring of the model's physical impressions
or visual outlay was probed before an artistic interpretation evolved.
Similarly, a structural impression or visual outlay of a model of design
activity emerged before an interpretive script was articulated.

A schema for an integrated model of engineering design was systematically elaborated from the "inside out," beginning at the center with the "core values" of design activity and then inductively working out from there, "layer by layer" (Mintzberg, 1994, p. 12). Mintzberg (1996) affirms that his thoughts on how to model human activity as an "evolving" phenomenon were shaped by his experiences as a doctoral student at the Sloan School of Management at MIT. In particular, his ideas for an "integrated" model "all came together, quite literally so in a framework of concentric circles." With the core values of design activity at the focal point of the model, the researcher could then bring into consideration the "milieu" ("thick description" or "rich context") in which these particular values are embedded. The core values act as "a kind of magnet" that holds the rest of the emerging model together, while the various themes are integrated around a framework of concentric circles. The circles act as a "permeable membrane" that stimulates "inner flow" among the themes of engineering design while allowing "outer flow" (Mintzberg, 1994, pp. 11-22) with the external environment that surrounds design activity.

Bohm's (1980) theory of the rheomode (or language) for express-

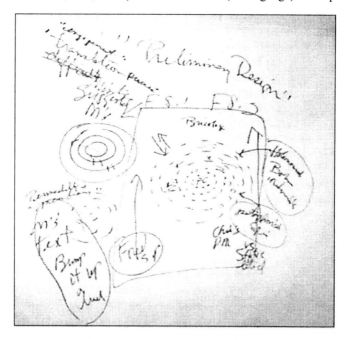

Figure 5.3. Emerging Schema for Engineering Design Activity in Its Visual and Messy Form (Copeland, p. 201)

ing "undivided wholeness in flowing movement" (p. xv) suggested an impression of elliptical instead of concentric circles surrounding design activity. The spontaneous, undefinable nature of these circles "create a new structure that is not so prone to fragmentation" (Bohm, p. 31) as traditional models based on concentric formats. The circles reflect the active, verbal nature of human problem-solving activity and "relevate" or lift up salient themes of design activity for the researcher. The holo-movement configuration "implies an unrestricted breadth and depth of meaning, that is not fixed within static limits" (Bohm, p. 35). It relevates or makes explicit the "whole implicate or enfolded order" (Bohm, p. 154) of engineering design.

After exploring Mintzberg's and Bohm's criteria for systematically structuring the design model, the researcher discovered a potential avenue for artistic interpretation of the phenomenon. Black (1962) asserts that all intellectual pursuits, including development of theoretical models, "rely firmly upon the imagination" (p. 242) of the researcher. The "heart of the method consists in 'talking' in a certain way [and seeing] new connections" for "rich, speculative" (pp. 228-237) interpretation of such models.

A dominant principle for a model of engineering design at this point is "isomorphism," the degree to which an artistic interpretation of the model can accurately capture the dominant themes of design activity. If a model is indeed a "heuristic fiction" (Black, p. 228) that points to a potential mode of interpretation, what is the artistic interpretation that can yield a "rich, speculative" narrative or script for describing engineering design?

According to Weber (1990), "time, effort, skill, and art are required to produce results, interpretations, and explanations that are theoretically 'interesting'" (p. 69) for engineering design. Hicks, Rush, and Strong (1985) state that the researcher's "imagination" is the driving force that stimulates the creative art of interpretation in inductive, content analysis techniques (p. 102). They consider the interpretive process a "practical art form ... motivated by the requirements of particular problem solving" (p. 478).

Weber asserts:

> Interpretation is in part an art. Those who naively believe that data or texts speak for themselves (the doctrine of radical empiricism) are mistaken. The content analyst contributes factual and theoretical knowledge to the interpretation. ...It is not the validity of an interpretation per se that is at issue, but rather the "salience" of an interpretation given

one or another theory. Just as it is true that quantitative data
do not speak for themselves (i.e., that the doctrine of radical empiricism is false), so is it true that texts do not speak
for themselves either. The investigator must do the speaking and the language of that speech is the language of theory [and model development]. (pp. 79-80)

The "salience" of an interpretation of engineering design must of
necessity be derived from the dominant themes of design activity, that
is, from the pragmatic and contingent themes of engineering design.
Cahoone (1997) stated that pragmatic and contingent patterns of engineering design as a human problem-solving process are "conceptually
promising clues" to an emerging postmodern interpretation of design
activity. In addition, the perspective of engineer as bricoleur would
provide the narrative text or supportive script for a visual model in this
context. Rorty (1997) indicated that a model of engineering design in-
terpreted through a postmodern lens of pragmatics and contingency
would be an "interesting" concept. Denzin (1995) implies that a postmodern or postfoundational approach is appropriate for interpreting the
"messy" data derived from qualitative research designs. This approach
"embraces" critical interpretations that are "always incomplete, personal, self-reflexive, and resistant to totalizing theories" (p. 183).

The pragmatic and contingent themes of design activity are the
core values for an artistic interpretation of engineering design—they
are the "magnetic core" that holds the other themes of design activity
together. The engineer as bricoleur engages in design activities that are
contingent upon the type of resources he/she may have on hand. The
engineer's method is an "emergent construction" (Weinstein and
Weinstein, 1991, p. 161) that changes and takes "new forms as different tools, methods, and techniques are added to the puzzle" (Lincoln
and Denzin, 1996, p. 2). In a context of ambiguity, paradox, and dissonance, the engineer as bricoleur understands that solutions to problems
are shaped by patterns of error and uncertainty. In particular, apparent
failure signals opportunity for "retooling." If new tools have to be in-
vented, or pieced together, then the engineer will do this. "Like the
bricoleurs of Lévi-Strauss," engineers often create solutions to problems with "makeshift equipment, spare parts, and assemblage" (Lincoln
and Denzin, 1996, p. 584). The choice of which tools to use and which
direction to move in solution space are not always set in advance.

The engineer is adept at intensive introspection that is sometimes
characterized by whimsical patterns of behavior. The product of the
engineer's labor is a bricolage, an artistic, "reflexive, collage-like crea-

tion" (Lincoln and Denzin, 1996, p. 3) that metaphorically represents the engineer's images, understandings, and interpretations of human problem solving. Bricolage is a pragmatic, practical solution to a given problem. It is often a satisficing, less than optimal solution that works in a given design context.

Following the positivist mode of thinking leaves no avenues to address the problems cited by Harris (1986), Blair (1990), and Laudan (1984). Indeed, there is an increasing sense of "incredulity" in the ability of a "legitimized scientific metanarrative" to solve these problems (Lyotard, 1979, pp. xxiv, 27). Wittgenstein's (1968) "perspicuous examples" are the critical link to understanding that information seeking is a pragmatic and contingent activity. Florman (1996) states that engineers are experiencing a "heightened level of awareness" that there are alternative modes for problem solving based on perspicuous examples of engineering design.

Postmodernism gives expression to some of these emerging modes of thinking. In particular, Foster (1985) illuminates the postmodern context that is appropriate for a model of engineering design as a human problem-solving activity. The "reactive" postmodern approach to problem solving involves "recycling old and discarded concepts—it deals in claimed certainties, 'the perfection of the past' or the 'past-perfect'—even though the past to which it refers is not the actual past but merely a nostalgic illusion of it" (p. 36). In contrast, the "resistive" version of postmodernism "deals with the real uncertainties of the world, 'the imperfect future' or 'future-imperfect.'" Where reactive postmodernism can never offer more than more of the same thing recycled, resistive postmodernism does at least offer the possibility of a "radically new understanding" of problem solution in a human context (Jackson and Carter, 1992, p. 16). Resistive postmodernism "inescapably presents itself as a new language" that can de-center the "albatross of scientific rationality" in problem solution (Foster, 1985, p. 13).

A resistive postmodern perspective involves the "fundamental questioning of a totalizing rationality based on science" (Jackson and Carter, 1992, p. 12). It illuminates potential problem-solving methods that "a dominant modernist style of thinking pushed into the shadows" (Cahoone, 1997).

Engineering, perhaps surprisingly, provides a substantive manifestation of resistive postmodern sensibilities. It "seeks not to recycle old [scientific] concepts" (Jackson and Carter, 1992, p. 16) as a reactive response to problem solution; instead, it is a resistive approach that explores the possibility of redefining the language and models of solution space. Engineering design, as a reflection of human activity and as a problem-solving epistemological entity freed from positivist assumptions, offers a means for getting us to "the right train station" and for determining which train to board.

There is a certain risk in giving a tidy and clean graphical expression to a nondeterministic model—one that presents messiness, emergence, and the numerous other attributes that made themselves evident in our examination of engineering design activity. Yet, so long as we remember that a model is but a way to grasp and manipulate concepts and constructs, such a graphic expression can be useful. Perhaps, in time, with different technology the temporal aspects and the permeable boundaries and the less-than-rigid relationships will be easier to present. Figure 5.4 is our current best attempt to translate the immediacy of figure 5.3 into a legible and coherent construct.

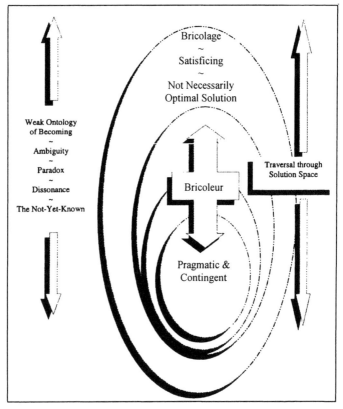

Figure 5.4. Nondeterministic Model of Engineering Design Activity, Adapted from Copeland

Chapter 6

Foraging for Relevance

Jodi Kearns

We are hunter-gatherers; there has not been enough evolutionary time for the hunter-gatherer brain to have changed. Recently, we have been able to articulate why and how we hunt and gather. Anthropologists concern themselves in-depth with the why in this puzzle. In the information-seeking realm, we can delineate a functional understanding. We hunt and gather, whether the hunting and gathering takes place on an online public access catalog or in a grocery store. The common thread is a notion in the hunter that something is lacking. In a very real sense we hunt and we forage for relevance.

There has been some confusion and controversy in the use of *hunting* and *gathering*, brought to our attention by a biologist colleague. It has been widely accepted that, historically, men hunted and women gathered. *To hunt* was to search for, kill, and process meat for the purposes of consuming calories, mastering techniques, and teaching youth. *To gather* was to find, collect, and use vegetation and other materials for food and for shelters, tools, and weapons. We use the terms here more generically to describe the hunt as the search and the gathering as the accumulation of information that, when applied, will bring one to some understanding or fulfillment. Definitions from the *Oxford English Dictionary* support our use of *hunting* and *gathering* in the information realm. Hunting and gathering are *the action of pursuing or searching* and *that which is drawn together; accumulation; union.*

These definitions imply a sequence one must follow. One searches and then one draws together relevant information. Our use of these terms is not dissimilar from the biological and historical use of our colleague. Essentially, from the points of view of both the biologist and the information scientist, hunting involves searching for something, consuming calories, mastering technique, and teaching. Likewise, gathering involves accumulating and using something in order to fill a certain need, whether the need is food, shelter, or new knowledge, regardless of gender. In fact new evidence shows that gender roles may well

have had less distinction in early societies than traditional models have
assumed (Pringle, 1998).

Relevance

The literature defines relevance richly and from a wide variety of philosophical stances. In short, the need for relevance leads hunter-
gatherers searching for whatever could solve the problem (Schamber,
1994). Whatever information solves the particular problem at a particular moment for a particular individual is relevant for that person in that
situation. Patrick Wilson (1973) describes situational relevance precisely in this manner. This could mean, then, that a cup of coffee is
relevant. (All who have experienced a throbbing caffeine headache can
attest to its relevance.) If the cup of coffee does not solve the problem
(get rid of the headache) then the search for more information, or relevance, continues. Perhaps relevance is not achieved until the hunter
gathers some acetaminophen tablets or seeks a quiet, dark place to grab
a nap.

Essentially, relevance can mean, by sheer weight of use, whatever
the hunter-gatherer wants it to mean. *Bearing upon the matter at hand*,
from the *Oxford English Dictionary*, demonstrates that whoever is concerned with the matter, or the problem, determines relevance. When
determining what is relevant for an individual, consider the following
taxonomic statement. Relevance is "what will answer the question …
what may suggest a way of answering the question … [or] what will
help one formulate what may turn out to be the answer one seeks"
(Wilson, 1968, p. 48). If the question is What's for supper? then relevance may be acquired respectively by the following: Pizza; I'm not
sure, let me call my mom; or Let's order out.

What Is *Question*?

There has been a long and rigorous attempt across the disciplines to
define *question*. In 1929, philosopher Felix Cohen compiled a system
of possible definitions and responses arguing the validity of each definition. A question could be a "request for information" (p. 352), but,
while this is generally true, Cohen points out that many questions are
presented with no intention of eliciting responses. Another view he
presents seeks to understand a question as an "ambiguous assertion" (p.
352). Cohen argues, however, that if by *ambiguous assertion* one

means "some kind of proposition, then no such assertion can be a question, since every proposition is either true or false and no question is either true or false" (p. 352). Instead of seeking a clear definition for question, which he demonstrates is like thinking in endless loops, Cohen settles on determining the nature of a question.

This nature of question seems to be what has been accomplished in the field of information studies also. More recently, Belkin (1982) thoroughly discusses an "anomalous state of knowledge" (often recognized by its clever acronym, ASK) in a set of papers. The anomaly indicates that one has at least a very slight notion that something is lacking. One seeks to fill, or give meaning to, whatever this anomaly represents. There is no doubt that question and relevance are related. Cohen (1929) and Wilson (1973) present similar arguments when they explain that whatever it is that may constitute a correct answer to, or give meaning to, or provide relevance for the anomalous state of one person may not fill the knowledge gap in another person with the same question.

Cohen makes a statement that seems simple and is presented almost in passing. He claims that "question is the beginning of thought" (p. 351). This definition, we believe, is his most significant, for it both implies a functional definition and describes the nature of question.[1] We see that all thoughts begin in question. The knowledge gap, or the anomalous state, spawns thought. Maron and Levien (1967) constructed a taxonomy of question types from the system perspective to aid their consideration of database design. O'Connor (1993) devised a taxonomy of question types from the seeker perspective. The two taxonomies can be merged into a matrix (MLO Matrix, for short) to describe the nature of question based on this idea that question is the beginning of thought (see figure 6.1).

One thinks about answering questions using degrees of depth required based on the complexity of the knowledge gap. These ways appear across the top of the MLO Matrix. As one moves along this horizontal axis, complexity of thought required and the set of possible answers increase.

	Look Up	Deductive Logic	Inductive Logic	Conversation
Articulated Query	LA	DA	IA	CA
Vague Awareness	LV	DV	IV	CV
Monitoring	LM	DM	IM	CM
Browsing	LB	DB	IB	CB
Encountering	LE	DE	IE	CE

Figure 6.1. Taxonomic Matrix of Question Types

Look Up refers to answers that can be found with a quick trip to the reference desk, or search engine. Around the reference desk, this type of question is often referred to as a ready-reference question. These are questions for which there tends to be a single or a very small set of agreed-upon answers. For example, How many birds are on the endangered species list for Kansas? *Deductive* and *Inductive Logic* are strategies for thinking about what may turn out to be the answer one seeks. The first strategy seeks to focus thinking down to a narrow set of possible answers, hopefully to a single answer, using the processes of formal logic; for example, the syllogism: Socrates is a man; all men are mortal; therefore Socrates is mortal. The second strategy accepts the possibility of a set of answers in an array of generalizations that may fill the knowledge gap. For example: 2, 4, 6, 8 … What's next? could yield either: "Who do we appreciate?" or "10, 12, 14" with equal validity; yet the set is small and based on experience. *Conversation* requires discussion and consultation of one or more sources in order to point to possible answers. There may never be an established and agreed-upon answer.

The vertical axis lists various question states or circumstances that one could discover beckoning attention. *Articulated Query* is a specified question; that is, the patron knows what is sought and how to phrase the query. *Vague Awareness* occurs when one has a dim notion of what the knowledge gap may be, but it cannot be precisely articulated (O'Connor, 1993). These two question states stem from a general perception that there is *something* one does not know. The remaining question states involve a realization that one does not know *everything* and one is open to and aware of incoming information. *Monitoring* occurs as one is constantly watching or scanning surroundings in anticipation of information that could stimulate thought (O'Connor, 1993); for example, always checking the new nonfiction book shelves or subscribing to a current contents service. *Browsing* is a strategy used to put oneself in a situation or circumstance, as in surrounding oneself with documents, in an attempt to shake up the knowledge store or to catch a glimpse of something new (O'Connor, 1993). *Encountering* happens when the new knowledge seemingly lands in one's lap without having actively gone out searching (Erdelez, 2000).

The purpose of the MLO Matrix is to pair a question state with a thought strategy for determining a relevant answer. As in the chart, an *Articulated Query* mapped to a *Look Up* strategy usually elicits a quick and simple response. The response to this particular question state using this particular thought strategy can be called an *LA* answer. For example, if the *Articulated Query* is Which is the deepest of the Great Lakes? and one applies the *Look Up* strategy and searches through the *Information Please* almanac, the *LA* answer would be Lake Superior. Similarly, each question state can be mapped to each thought strategy and relevant answers can most certainly reduce, if not fill, the knowledge gap. A *Conversational* strategy applied to an *Articulated Query* would result in a *CA* answer. What is the prettiest lake in Canada? is a well-articulated question requiring conversation to determine an answer since subjectivity may intervene.

Various question states or question circumstances, though they fit nicely into the MLO Matrix, may have, in reality, no algorithmic connection. Mapping them into the MLO Matrix may direct one toward discovering the relevance one seeks. Question states and the search for relevance overwhelm all who hunt and gather. Outlining possible question states and degrees of relevance simply helps express the essential need and what can be done to satisfy it.

Relevance for Hunter-Gatherers

We are *all* hunter-gatherers. Recent studies have shown "the existence, some 300,000 years ago, of mental ability equivalent to that of modern man" (Gamble, 1980, p. 522). Gamble also posits that *information*, not simply the human brain, has been evolving since the existence of our earliest ancestors; humans, of course, are the contributors to this form of evolution. This is not to say that we have not physically evolved in appearance over the past 300,000 years. We have. Our brains, however, have long had the capacity to achieve, analyze, think, and plan in the manner we do today.

Whether thousands of years ago or today, hunter-gatherers have suffered anomalous states of knowledge and sought relevance. Perhaps thousands of years ago Cro-Magnon (modern hunter-gatherers—us) wondered when the herd would next migrate, so that they might hunt and then gather food for their families. The anomalous state was the uncertainty about the next meal. They sought relevance by employing the technology of weaponry, tools, and communication and harvesting the kill. Modern hunter-gatherers are not dissimilar. The anomalous state could range from Where is the bathroom? to What is for supper? to How do I unclog the drain? to How do I prove the hypothesis of my dissertation? Relevance is achieved by foraging for answers.

Our anomalous states can be anything that we feel is missing from our knowledge stores. Our anomalous states could be the same as that of early hunter-gatherers. For example, we have a need to ingest and digest food. How we choose to satiate this need is situationally relevant. Fortunately, we do not have to achieve gaining our food calories in the same manner as Cro-Magnon or Neanderthal—though some may choose to, usually as a hobby. We can go to the grocery store. Grocery shopping is optimal foraging. Just about anything that we need is located at the grocery store. We use the same hunting and gathering strategies and tactics that humans have been using for thousands of years, and this is no coincidence.

Many times we also have needs that are not so basic and fundamental to our physical survival. For instance, students, scholars, and professionals have information needs. Depending on the depth of the knowledge we are seeking, our relevance for these situations varies.

Foraging

Describing *why* we hunt and gather is challenging. For our purpose, which does not include the explanation of the anatomy and physiology of the human brain that drives our natural instincts, we hunt and gather because we have a particular need that we are attempting to fill. Describing *how* we accomplish this is simpler because we can observe hunting and gathering behaviors in ourselves.

To clarify with the help of the *Oxford English Dictionary*, foraging is "roving in search of provisions." This definition is consistent with what appears to be a recurring theme among those who talk about the forage for relevance. Carl Sagan notes that ancient Egyptians called the library "nourishment for the soul" (Sagan, 1989); others talk about the "flavors of relevance" (Pai, in O'Connor, 1996); and still others pilgrimage toward feeding a spiritual hunger. Foraging and relevance seem to somehow be linked to an inherent need for nourishment. One could say foraging provides sustenance for body, mind, and soul. Optimizing the nourishment is a task that has challenged hunter-gatherers since our beginning.

Optimal Foraging

Optimal foraging is an established biological and anthropological theory that plots searching and handling curves on cost and benefits axes to determine their relationship. It surmises that we are continuously looking for ways to optimize searching techniques. The search is considered the time the forager spends looking for prey. Handling begins with the forager's decision to pursue, and includes the capture, the processing, and the consumption (Sandstrom, 1999). Cost is considered the number of calories expended in the forage for a particular item. Benefits are considered the number of calories gained by the use of the item. In Cro-Magnon's life, search cost would have been high after spending two days hunting and coming home with a single rabbit. Benefits would have been low, since many calories were expended for this harry (or hairy) return.

The cost-benefit idea also applies to library research. If a student spends three hours searching through literature databases for articles on a certain topic, and very few hits are returned, search cost is high and benefits are low. Or when several hits result from a quick database search, and the Online Public Access Catalog (OPAC) tells the student that the item is "available." An hour may be spent navigating through the stacks trying to locate the desired item. Finally the student determines the item is missing, despite what the OPAC indicated. The student leaves the library with nothing. Search cost was high; benefits were low.

Suppose the search had been successful. The student's first search returned several hits and each item was indeed in the collection. Then search cost was low and benefits were high. The 1980s saw the change from card-catalog searching to OPAC searching. During card-catalog searching, one had no option to use keywords to articulate a search query. Patrons were accustomed to searching by subject, and most continued to do so on the online catalog. At first, very few ventured to try keyword searching. Within a decade, keyword searching increased and subject searching became as useless to patrons on OPACs as keyword searching was to patrons in the card catalog. This is not surprising, since keyword searching and OPACs have on the whole provided a better cost-to-gain ratio.

Optimal foraging attempts to expend the fewest calories possible for the greatest benefit during the combined efforts for searching and handling. The idea is to bring the apex (indicated with the arrow) to such a position that benefits for searching and handling are high and cost is low (Churchill, 1998). While such optimization may be the goal of automation, it has yet to be achieved (Borgman, 1996).

In the literature of evolutionary ecology and anthropology, optimal foraging contains the same fundamental elements:

a) an *actor* (defined as an individual organism) that pursues or chooses alternative strategies and tactics;
b) a *strategy* that identifies available options;
c) a *currency* that defines and analyzes the cost-benefit structure and measurement of gain available;
d) a set of *constraints* in which the strategies and payoffs are determined (Smith and Winterhalder, 1992).

This method can be seamlessly applied to hunter-gatherers who are seeking any type of resource, or attempting to fill a gap in their knowledge stores. Depending on the particular need, an actor may be on a general search for something that will fill the gap. Other times, the forager is on a more determined quest and will bypass many other types of information, food, calories, and so on, in order to satisfy a more specific or articulated need.

Three Ways to Optimize

In order to optimize, an actor's goal is to alter the total search cost by gaining many calories in turn for processing an item. In a presentation for the Institute of Human Origins, Steve Churchill explains three means of optimization, or lowering search cost for high-ticket items: wild harvesting, creating information systems, and planning depth.

Wild harvesting involves cooperative hunting methods in order to turn a field of large animals into meals for several months. He claims Neanderthal people (early Homo sapiens mono-strategic hunter-gatherers) would have seen the field-full and thought *Dinner!*—not *five months of secured meals*. Creating information systems involves some planning. If the size and location of the herd can be narrowed down, then the right labor group can be prepared and sent to hunt. Other people are integral to working information systems. Planning depth of the information network optimizes foraging further. The more that is known before the hunt, the better prepared the hunters will be, and the fewer calories will be expended. Cro-Magnon reduced search cost by planning, and they made low-cost bulk caloric inputs possible.

Optimal foraging is not functional only for explaining survival success and extinction in early hominids. If one equates calories to information (Campbell, 1982) (which is not a far leap if one recalls the First Law of Thermodynamics where energy can be neither created nor destroyed, just converted), there are interesting implications for modern hunter-gatherers and the ways we search, or our attempt to gain the most information with the lowest search cost.

Foraging Tactics

Tactics move a search forward. In *Information Search Tactics* (1979b), Marcia Bates articulates six foraging tactics, as seen in the following chart (figure 6.2). Bates describes how these (and other) tactics can be applied both to bibliographic searches in which one seeks bibliographic citations to documents that will contain information one desires and to reference searches in which one searches to find information to answer a specific question.

One can observe that these same tactics are, often unconsciously, applied to foraging in common, everyday situations. We use the same tactics, for example, while foraging in the grocery store, as posed in figure 6.3.

In addition to the tactics Bates described, we observed another tactical strategy. Occasionally, one encounters information that, though it does not answer any pressing questions, seems valuable. One tucks it away because it may come in handy later. This may be what the scholar does when she spots an intriguing book in the new acquisitions shelf at the library. It could help one formulate what may turn out to be the answer one seeks. This save-it-for-later tactic assumes planning ahead, or at least knowing that one may require some planning at another time. Seeds, an article, or Y2K supply of instant rice: the effect is the same. This save-it-for later tactic assumes that one may find a piece of information useful, though not immediately pertinent, and saves it for later, anticipating that this tidbit might move a yet unknown search forward.

Hunter-gatherers, by nature, store information for use, understanding that there may be a time when information is scarce.

---

specify: to search on terms that are as specific as the information

exhaust: to include most or all elements of the query in the initial search formulation; to add one or more of the query elements to an already prepared search formulation

reduce: to minimize the number of elements of the query in the initial search formulation; to subtract one or more of the query elements from an already prepared search formulation

parallel: to make the search formulation broad by including synonyms or otherwise conceptually parallel terms

pinpoint: to make the search formulation precise by minimizing the number of parallel terms, retaining the more perfectly descriptive terms

block: to reject, in the search formulation, items containing certain terms, even if it means losing some sections of relevance

Adapted from Bates (1979b)

Figure 6.2. Foraging Tactics

Foraging Strategies

Tactics move the search forward, and strategies are the search methods employed to execute the hunt. One can observe foraging strategies in action in everyday situations. Several foraging strategies are defined in the following descriptions. Any of the strategies can be used to forage for whatever relevance is being sought. The strategy employed depends on one's depth within the search process and the specificity of information that is required.

---

specify: I want Land-o-Lakes, Morning Blend margarine.

exhaust: I want cottage cheese, large curds, low fat.

reduce: Since there is no low-fat, large-curd cottage cheese, I'll take any large-curd cottage cheese.

parallel: I need acetaminophen; Tylenol or generic brands will do.

pinpoint: I need Tylenol.

block: I want potato chips, not BBQ, salt and vinegar, or rippled.

Figure 6.3. Foraging Tactics Applied to Grocery Shopping

Hunting and Picking

Hunting is predicting the likeliest location to find a useful item (P. Wilson, 1968). Imprecision in representations of document sets still plagues information seekers of disabling item specificity. The hunter has narrowed the search by predicting the likeliest location. If representations were specific, single bibliographic records would be at least as lengthy as the document itself. Each word, idea, and dog-ear would be necessary to provide definite identification of each item, rendering the catalog redundant and useless. An accompanying strategy is necessary to identify relevant documents. *Picking* is selecting items based on a description when the description is imprecise (Wilson, 1968), narrowing the possible solutions set further. Presumably, the purpose of bibliographic tools (indexes, abstracts, bibliographies) is to minimize the amount of hunting and picking a forager needs in order to find relevant information. In the library, professionals have tried to create systems of representations to reduce hunting and picking. Essentially, these professionals have attempted to reduce search cost for patrons. Hunting on the World Wide Web may often prove to be a futile enterprise, as likely locations are frequently impossible to predict. The search engine Google.com provides an *I Feel Lucky* search option that, allowing one to feel like the possibilities are not infinite, takes the searcher to what the algorithm decides is the best fit for the search. In typical Web searches, one must pick through hits to discover what one wishes to have hunted in the beginning.

Coupling

Coupling is an extension of Wilson's ideas on hunting and picking (1968). It involves generating links between what one hunted and picked. Coupling supposes that the forager has focused the likeliest location of the resources (hunted) and has gathered the seemingly relevant documents (picked), but has not generated any links between the question state and what has been hunted and picked. We consider this process a foraging strategy in how one might use coupling to search tidbits that have been stored in a save-it-for-later tactic for what may fill a knowledge gap. In this way, it is possible for one to couple one's own thoughts. One might assimilate and accommodate new knowledge, or draw connections from current knowledge stores that have not yet been linked.

Indexing

Indexing points to what has a reasonable likelihood of being relevant (O'Connor, 1996). Bibliographies point to resources that may also pertain to the topic of the bibliography, for example, and maps point to where one might need to be. A forager uses an index, of whatever sorts, to direct the search or to point the search in the direction of what could be the relevant target. Back-of-the-book indexes reduce search time and cost by directing the search in what could be the right direction. An index, no matter the intent of the indexer, can be useful only insofar as it points to what the forager needs (Wilson, 1968). The optimal index, then, is only situationally relevant to individual foragers.

Browsing

Browsing is hunting for sustenance in an area where finding and evaluating resources are issues. It is foraging for an unknown among uncertainties (O'Connor, 1993); it tends to have a high cost-to-gain ratio. If the library was filled with volumes of unorganized documents, then this could be a browsable collection. Just as an animal might browse to satisfy a need for nourishment without knowing what shape the anticipated nourishment might take, browsing can be a response to subject indeterminacy (O'Connor, 1996) when a basic unarticulated need for information exists. Even in an organized collection, if the collection is not organized to the specific requirements of a particular user, browsing may be a necessary hunting strategy. The browser anticipates, or is open to, discovering an answer somewhere in the wilderness through which he forages.

Grazing

Similar to browsing, *grazing* is foraging in a space where evaluation and supply are not issues. Grazing is foraging among knowns or certainties (O'Connor, 1988, 1996) and there is a lower cost-to-gain ratio. One grazes when one forages in an area where a subject is determined, as in the library stacks. It is common knowledge that grazing around 398.2 in a Dewey classified system is a place to find stories of traditional and folk lore. Even if unfamiliar with the classification system, one can be fairly certain that, at any random point in the stacks, the documents on either side of the point share some common subject. Items in such places have been preevaluated and presupplied for grazers such as ourselves. The same is true of grocery stores, hardware stores, video stores, pastures, and barnyards, which are all designed (evaluated and stocked) to foster grazing. Next time a clerk at the video store asks, "Can I help you find something?" the appropriate response would be, "No thank you, I'm just grazing." If an animal browses for a place to feed and returns to the same spot the very next day, does it on the second day graze since the feeding spot has been preevaluated, or does it browse since the possibility exists that the supply may not be there on the next day? Grazing implies that some other force is responsible for ensuring supply, like the farmer, the librarian, or the manager of the video store.

Berrypicking

Berrypicking originated with the idea that huckleberries are spread out over bushes. The berrypicker must pick one at a time before moving on to the next berry, since the berries are scattered throughout the forest. This idea was originally applied to online search techniques (Bates, 1989b). The idea is that any online search is an evolving search. One could not employ berrypicking without the query evolving. One searches when one has some sort of question state. When presented with documents that prove to be relevant, one reads and decides if the question has been answered. If it has not been answered, the question has inevitably been changed by the new knowledge, and an evolving question is prompted. The forager continues to berrypick until an answer is reached and the search thread is ended. Anyone who has done berrypicking can recall ending far from the original thought on the original webpage, as such is the nature of evolving ideas.

Glimpsing

The idea that the human eye catches similarities between the knowledge gap and the surrounding information as the eye moves across an area is *glimpsing*. Perception is a sequence of glimpses and each glimpse conveys a "pittance of information" (Morse, 1973, p. 247). One with a known or unknown question state may or may not be searching for relevance when glimpses have been caught. The bit of information caught in a glimpse may fill a current gap or it may be filed away and saved for later. The objective is to optimize the number of glimpses in order to increase the probability of catching a useful glimpse. Glimpsing is extremely useful in noticing bargains at the grocery store. Optimal foraging shoppers optimize glimpses to lower search cost both of calories and of dollars.

Expert Hunting

This foraging strategy might also be called *intuitive hunting*, because this name implied the ability of the forager to make predictions based on expertise incurred from experience. Intuition leads the forager to the location where the information will be. "The Great One," Wayne

Gretzky, attributed his hockey success to an intuition that guided him to skate to where the puck was going to be.

The same sort of intuition guides the expert hunter. Dreyfus and Dreyfus (1986) describe five stages one manifests along the journey from novice to expert: novice, advanced beginner, competence, proficiency, and expertise. By the time one becomes an expert, one has incorporated all the information of the other phases into such a full understanding that the ideas become part of the expert's quintessence. "Experts don't solve problems and don't make decisions; they do what normally works" (Dreyfus and Dreyfus, 1986, p. 31). Expert hunters go to where the puck will be; they go to where the relevant documents are; they go to where the answer is known. In an interview (presented in chapter 3) with Gary McAlister (called Gary Mac in his squadron), a retired submarine chaser in the U.S. Navy, we learned that achieving expertise is common with those who have foraged intuitively, gathering knowledge and building knowledge stores of the target. He agrees with the submarine chaser in *The Hunt for Red October:* "It's wise to study the ways of one's adversary."

Satisficing

Satisficing can be considered a form of settling. It often finds foragers settling for what information is most readily available with little or no regard for cost and benefits. All hunter-gatherers are prone to satisficing rather than optimizing at times that require quick, and possibly temporary, answers to immediate questions. It is in this same light that the *Oxford English Dictionary* defines satisficing: "To decide on and pursue a course of action that will satisfy the minimum requirements necessary to achieve a particular goal." Remember the grocery store analogy and consider this example. Someone in search of Tylenol runs into a convenience store for a quick headache remedy. In choosing this type of store, this person is satisficing. The customer is there for no other reason than to get the one thing that will help his headache go away. The customer neither wants nor needs anything else at this time. By doing so, he is not optimizing. If the convenience store that he chose does not carry Tylenol, he will probably choose any parallel acetaminophen product, and not choose to find another location that sells Tylenol. The customer is satisficing by obtaining the minimum requirement necessary to achieve his goal. Perhaps this could be a more reasonable example if the product being sought was diapers, or condoms.

In the Navy, the Construction Battalion (CBs or Sea Bees) would be called in to build a bridge that would need to support fifty trucks passing over a river. What happened to it after everyone crossed did not matter. They were not finding an optimal solution, just a satisfying one. There may be no way of knowing optimization within satisficing, and this is alright.

Bricolage

Like satisficing, the *bricoleur* is the person who can use whatever information is readily available to satisfy the need (Copeland, 1997; Lévi-Strauss, 1966). The answer is found by coupling whatever resources are currently available. It involves making sense of thoughts. On the physical side, the bricoleur can build gadgets from ready pieces and can improvise on building materials in order to fix a broken faucet. Bricolage is foraging for whatever works from information or materials at hand. It is doing what we can with what we have.

Collaborating

Collaborating is a cooperative effort put forth by those foraging in order to lower the search cost. It involves team planning. Consider the team situations within the military where effective collaboration is executed. They use the same tactics that were described earlier in order to achieve what is relevant to them and their situations. In the interview with Gary McAlister (October 1998), the retired submarine hunter with the U.S. Navy, collaboration is imperative in the quest to find a submarine. Often, he admits, one must collaborate with oneself. Gary Mac refers to his past experiences and his vast knowledge stores that he gained from watching and listening to other experts. Collaboration with the pilot, as is evident in his interview, is particularly essential. Both must want to move the search forward and exert the energy that is necessary. In the library, similar collaborative efforts could be used to minimize search cost. Patrons collaborate with themselves during the resurfacing of prior knowledge and the articulation of the question of a skilled search. Collaboration occurs in the library between the librarian and the patron, patrons and other library users, and even between the cataloger and the patron (even though the collaboration is not simultaneous). The distribution of expenditures of the energy in collaboration results is beneficial with a sufficient return of calories.

Handling

Handling is the decision to pursue, capture, process, and consume (Smith and Winterhalder, 1992). Handling costs need to consider all four of these events. The actor must be willing to expend all of the required calories that will be used in this sequence of events in order to achieve the desired goal. A cost-benefit analysis is mandatory. A bounty hunter does precisely this—is willing to expend many calories to find his information and achieve his goal. Cost is high in a multi-thread search with many dead ends. Although a handler may encounter many morsels of what may turn out to be useless information, benefits are high. The same is true of the student who enters the library one hour before closing and needs to write a legible and intelligible paper for the next morning.

Scavenging

Scavenging is "to thieve, to borrow, to pick through leftovers," according to the *Oxford English Dictionary*. It is a strategy that does not require one to exert much effort; handling cost is low. It is a sort of simplified satisficing. Although when an actor chooses to employ scavenging as a strategy, it does not necessarily mean that he is intending to satisfy minimum requirements to achieve a known goal. Scavenging is a strategy applied by many students to acquire information based on assumed educative judgments of higher academics. It is a way of gathering facts, and producing a paper without stating any personal opinions. "Carnivores scavenge when they can and hunt when they must" (Leakey, 1994, p. 72). One could say scavenging is the precursor to creative thought. Before one can properly articulate thoughts and criticisms, one must pick through leftovers and borrow thoughts that others have gathered. Sometimes we wish more people would scavenge for ideas before prejudging.

Tracking

When an animal has no information about the location of resources in the environment, it moves so as to optimize its chances of locating resources and to reduce the chances of revisiting (Bell, 1991). Some people depend on storm trackers who monitor local atmospheric action and forecast weather. Others track for recreation through the wilderness to find shelter, food, and water. And still others use a wilderness to track. The World Wide Web can seem to be a wilderness to some users in the sense that it is a confusing multitude of networks of information and a bewildering situation for some. We now have the capability to track online. We can follow packages, planes, and mail in order to maintain knowledge of location. We have learned that search efficiency improves when one uses sensory cues to locate information. We should follow the example of the bloodhound who among animals is an olfactory giant. The bloodhound does not gather scents in a single line beginning at one point and ending victoriously at the target. Rather, it makes grand sweeps to either side of the trail in order to track the desired information without revisiting. The path from a question to an answer is not usually a straight one.

Sitting and Waiting

A widely accepted predation strategy is known as sit-and-wait. The anglerfish, horned frogs, and spiders are examples of animals that use sit-and-wait predation. Essentially, such a predator finds a place to sit where prey is likely to pass by, waits, and as prey nears, it comes out to feed. Spiders snare insects on a web; horned frogs dwell in streams where the fish and insect populations are high. These predators expend minimal calories in search, and caloric intakes can be minimal. Sandstrom (1999) discusses information as prey. If by *prey* one means the victim under pursuit and attack with no ability to resist, it is not a giant leap in correlating what an anglerfish does in its environment and what an information seeker does in the library. One cannot help receiving information by just sitting and waiting by means of radio, television, headlines on articles in grocery store checkouts, or junk mail. Sit-and-wait foraging in humans can prove to be an effective way to intercept information one may or may not be anticipating. But forager be warned: this may not be a wise strategy to adopt as one's sole source of information income! Churchill (1996) suggests that sit-and-wait predation might account for the demise of Neanderthal, who dwelled in caves and hunted only when prey was spotted running past.

Wading in the Stream

If we are hunter-gatherers and we are accustomed to walking around card catalogs, then the problem with World Wide Web and OPAC searching is that we are looking at a single point in a huge stream of data on a flat screen. We cannot wade into the stream; we merely see the surface in front of us; we are not sure of where we are along the stream's length; or how deep the stream may be; or what rocks and logjams create both challenges and opportunities. We might say the challenge is to attempt to reinvent ways to step back into the stream's currents; to enable standing high enough to see the source or the local configuration; to judge the depth; to reintegrate tactility and space into the physical data stream of the single-screen interface.

A Closing Thought

We close our overview of our hunter-gatherer nature with two comments from Patrick Wilson (1968), an admonition and a description of the good hunter in the academic library setting.

> Of course even the wisest hunter and picker cannot be certain of finding all there is to find; we may, by hunting and picking, in fact find all there is to find, but we cannot know that we have done so. (p. 105)

> The good hunter is one with a good deal of accumulated knowledge and experience of the history and habits of scholars, of the fashions and tendencies of thought and investigation, the preferences and predilections of scholars of different ages and traditions, all of which knowledge and experience he uses, perhaps without conscious formulation in his estimates of likelihood. (p. 112)

Chapter 7

Prologue to Dialectic

Brian O'Connor, Jud Copeland, and Jodi Kearns

Colloquia and conversations need not end with tidy summaries and models. We have taken the liberty of using *prologue* rather than *conclusion* or *epilogue*, seeing our efforts as a type of catalytic prologue to initiate discourse in the field on the current state of information studies and the role of the physical self in seeking behavior. One of the fundamental purposes of our colloquy is to initiate some discourse as a direct response to Michael Harris's apologia about the *dialectic of defeat* mentality that exists in our field (Harris, 1986). As the field continues to build on interdisciplinarian- or multidisciplinarian-flavored paralogies, it is incumbent upon us as accountable and responsible information scientists to initiate that discourse. We hope that within the preceding pages there have emerged threads of ideas of some significance to our colleagues actively engaged in using, designing, or evaluating human information-seeking behavior. We also hope that current and horizon technologies for collegial interaction will enable the continuation, expansion, and weaving of these conversational threads into a more robust conception of humans in their information environment.

We began with a curiosity over observations of distress over the abandonment of the paper card catalog and observations of people seeking information and things outside the ordinary realm of information-seeking studies. We contemplated the current state of information studies and looked to engineering and postmodern sensibilities to illuminate what might be in the shadows of our understanding. These caused us to consider the role of the physical self in seeking behavior.

Thinking of the physical self illuminated an intriguing paradigmatic couplet and its situation in the digital era. It would not be unduly facile to suggest that the primary formal bibliographic apparatus has an epistemological base linked to Aristotle. Fairly rigid categories and constrained assumptions about seeking behavior (or at least the sorts of behavior that could be supported; see Svenonius, 2000) arose over the centuries of modern librarianship both from world views of the dominant players and from the constraints of paper documents. Within this environment, until recently, library users have operated within a physical environment hospitable to their hunter-gatherer heritage. They walked through stacks, they pulled drawers from cabinets, they knew: *I am in the Cs now and the Ws are over there.*

The digital environment has fostered the reverse situation for users. A variety of search engines provides numerous ways to re-arrange the documents in a collection; chat rooms and list-servs expand the number of near neighbors we may consult; works from around the world may be available with a few keystrokes. Thus, we might say, the document environment is hospitable to the inductive, dynamic, idiographic (in the sense of "one's own, pertaining to oneself") associative processes characteristic of much human activity. Yet, at the same time, we have no physical connection with or sense of the size or arrangement of the document space. We may know we *are here now,* but have no sense of *how much is between here and there, wherever there is.* We have yet, on a large scale, to bring into play both the physical engagement with the environment and the intellectual dynamics that have served hominids for so long.

Supporting one of our primary theses—the poverty of the Aristotelian model—is the almost stunning passage from the introduction to Damasio's investigation into neurology and the nature of being, *Descartes' Error: Emotion, Reason, and the Human Brain* (1995, p. xi):

> I began writing this book to propose that reason may not be as pure as most of us think it is or wish it were, that emotions and feelings may not be intruders in the bastion of reason at all; they may be enmeshed in its networks for better or worse.

Science writer David Berreby (2001) makes a comment that addresses the hunter-gatherer nature of those whose stories we have related and links them to information work:

> [P]eople who trade in information behave more like hunter-gatherers and less like our immediate ancestors, who were chained to the plow and the factory. People who succeed in an information economy are alert and adaptable to an ever-changing environment. They work in small groups. They are independent thinkers who dislike taking orders, and they are fervently egalitarian. They place their faith in face-to-face relationships, not in authority or title. As long as humanity made its living in agriculture or industry, such

> traits were suppressed in favor of those more amenable to centralization, obedience to authority, long chains of command.
>
> This epoch is coming to an end. The Postindustrial West no longer values stability, steadfastness, and predictability over change, adaptability, and flexibility....Business people often remark that their twenty-something employees can't take orders and expect to be able to dress as they please and bring their parrot to work.

Note here the connection to Leakey and others regarding early hominid development as an adaptation to rapidly changing environments, such as the Great Rift Valley. Note the close connection with bounty hunter O'Connor's motto: "Resist Much, Obey Little."

Gary Mac (see chapter 3) studied books and maps and charts and instruments. He *knew* weather, ocean currents, seafloor topography, and the abilities of Soviet submarines. When he speaks in person of his submarine chasing, his face lights up as he remembers his old mentors and companions, not just because they were nice people with whom to associate, but because they helped him. When he speaks of chasing a Soviet sub for mission after mission and finally catching it, Gary clenches his fist, yanks it toward his body, and growls, "Gotcha!"

The bounty hunter knows information sources and the habits of skip tracers. When he speaks of his work he fairly winces at the nights spent sitting in cars just hoping to catch a glimpse of someone; he becomes animated relating the terror and utter thrill of chasing someone who might shoot back; he clenches his fist and exclaims, "No way that sucker was getting away!"

The discussion of engineering design epistemology likewise brought us to the very physical world. We heard of feeling it in our bones; of a discipline founded directly in the earliest days of our species; of solving real-world problems.

Analysis of these stories and the application of a postmodern lens demonstrate that Information Science may have been barking up the wrong metaphor. Rorty's (1991) theory of pragmatics and Lévi-Strauss's (1966) concept of "bricolage" provide strong links between our hunter and gatherer nature, engineering design, and the urgent crises of Information Science. The engineering—bricolage—pragmatics metaphor turns the Kuhnian crisis "Are we a science?" on its head.

Iteration and a capacity for time-varying events, collaboration, pattern recognition, and reasoning for action (operate on incomplete data, analogical, inductive) together with the thrill of the hunt (Sagan and Druyan, 1993) are the primary attributes that emerged. These are the very sorts of attributes we saw emerge from Copeland's analysis of engineering design (chapter 5). It is, then, not surprising that we would suggest the resistive postmodern model of engineering as a starting place for expanding notions of seeking behavior. *Mens et Manus* is the motto that accompanies the reader and the blacksmith on the emblems of the Massachusetts Institute of Technology, reminding us of the deep intertwining of mind and hand. The possibility of an epistemological model hospitable to ambiguity, respectful of failures, and aware that passions are full partners of reason emerged from our conversations.

We make no pretense of having a complete version of a model of information-seeking behavior or a complete set of attributes for each and every information retrieval system. Indeed, the postmodern engineering approach would likely eschew any attempt to compose either. We can summarize our stories and make assertions based on those stories about a "functional focus" for designers and for those who are engaged in information-seeking behaviors. The final model and assertions emerge from our stories. We have presented a multilayered model and included brief comments on the emergent assertions, less for full explication than for provoking thought along lines beyond our stories.

Layers of a Schema

	Look Up	Deductive Logic	Inductive Logic	Conversation
Articulated Query	LA	DA	IA	CA
Vague Awareness	LV	DV	IV	CV
Monitoring	LM	DM	IM	CM
Browsing	LB	DB	IB	CB
Encountering	LE	DE	IE	CE

Figure 7.1. Matrix of Information-Seeking Strategies

We return to earlier models as a foundation. First, the model of question types and question states set into a matrix of information-seeking strategies is presented in figure 7.1. In this matrix, we see that as we move away from the well-articulated look-up-question state, the more likely we are to see more complex, contingent, iterative, and collaborative-seeking behavior. Second, we layer onto this our functional, pragmatic, emergent, contingent, and satisficing model constructed earlier and presented on page 116.

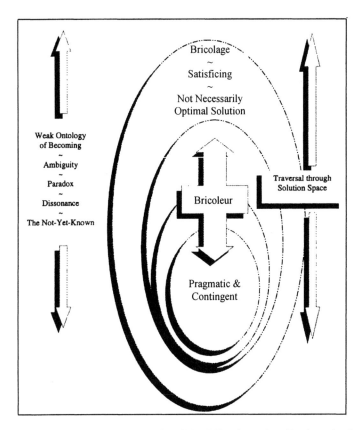

Figure 7.2. Nondeterministic Model of Engineering Design Activity, Adapted from Copeland

This foundational element of our model of the emergent approach to seeking behavior is: functional, pragmatic, contingent, and satisficing.

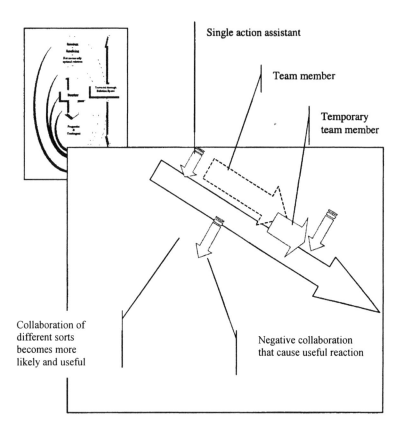

Single action assistant

Team member

Temporary
team member

Collaboration of
different sorts
becomes more
likely and useful

Negative collaboration
that cause useful reaction

Figure 7.3. First-Level Elaboration

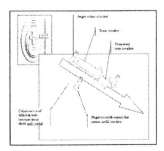

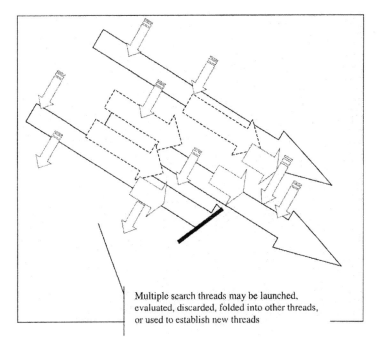

Multiple search threads may be launched,
evaluated, discarded, folded into other threads,
or used to establish new threads

Figure 7.4. Second-Level Elaboration

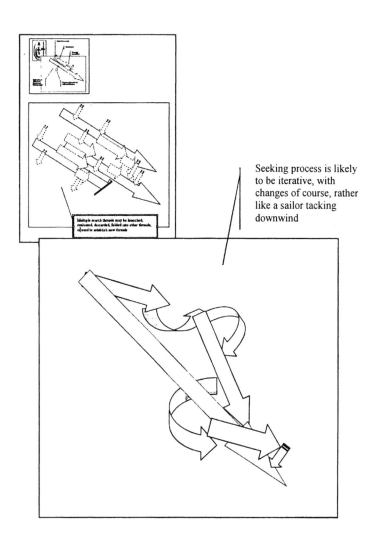

Seeking process is likely to be iterative, with changes of course, rather like a sailor tacking downwind

Figure 7.5. Third-Level Elaboration

Table 7.1. Assertions

- Acknowledges, enables *less than optimal* or *satisficing* target
- Acknowledges collaborative, social seeking behavior
- Acknowledges role of failure in making progress
- Recognizes iterative nature of seeking and questioning
- Recognizes iterations may take place over multiple sessions
- Recognizes multithreaded tactics
- Recognizes generate, test, regenerate evaluation and feedback
- Relieves burden of representation on system or cataloger
- Shifts role of information professional to authority on achieving functional retrieval

We assert that the case stories, contemplations, and conversations enable us to posit some assertions about information-seeking behavior. These are summarized in table 7.1 and elaborated below. Again, these are touchstones for consideration, rather than necessary attributes or guidelines.

Allows, acknowledges, enables less than optimal or satisficing target: here we recognize the value of what has been a long-standing situation at the reference desk. A patron with some question engages the librarian. If the query can be articulated, the librarian seeks some appropriate documents, only to find the most appropriate is checked out. A reasonable response has been "The one I really wanted you to have is already checked out, but these two should give you a good start, and they have some excellent illustrations." In the event the query is one of the many sorts in the matrix of question types for which there may not be a ready single response, the librarian may make a few forays into parts of the collection with potential, select some samples, and go through a generate-test-regenerate sequence with the patron until a useful work is found.

Acknowledges collaborative, social nature of seeking behavior: collaboration is at the heart of many human endeavors, even those that seem on the surface to be lone ventures. We offer a brief taxonomy of collaborative activities:

- Team hunt (many with similar skills and group plan)
- Team hunt (many with different skills and group plan)
- Occasional contact by lone seeker—updates and feedback
- Group agreement that lone hunter is appropriate to task.

There are forms of engagement with others that are less formal and obvious, yet bear mentioning here. Mentors may be said to collaborate in an unconstrained time frame. The lessons learned, the habits of proceeding and evaluating, and the passions are elements that would not be available in their current state without past collaboration. We might speak of self-reflection in a similar manner; looking back on one's past hunts and accomplishments constitutes a form of collaboration with oneself. A very different form of collaboration generally has pejorative terms attached to it. Increased passion from negative encounters may be the best way to characterize it. Think back to the submarine chaser being determined to demonstrate that arrogant superior officers were wrong. Think back to the bounty hunter re-doubling his efforts in the face of legal quibblings over jurisdictional issues.

Acknowledges role of failure in making progress: failure to come across a helpful document may not be a very pleasant experience for either the seeker or the managers of a document collection (especially if the economic viability of the enterprise rests on search success). However, examining why people are leaving a session disappointed or why they leave satisfied only to discover later that the documents in hand are actually of little assistance can refine the processes for the next iteration. It is, of course, one thing to say *embrace failure*, and quite another to establish and operate within an environment that does so also. The elementary school student who comes to school without a report on the due day may have a difficult time saying to the teacher, "I didn't find any good material on the topic area even though I spent a lot of time, but I did learn a lot about searching the Web that should help me do a great job later in the week."

Recognizes iterative nature of seeking and question development and that iterations may take place over multiple sessions: the phenomenon of a solution coming to one in the shower or out on a canoe trip after weeks of wrestling with ideas is linked to Hapgood's concept of *stuckness*. Sometimes one has to reach a point of exhaustion sufficient to drop preconceptions; sometimes one simply has to conduct many generate-test-regenerate trials; sometimes an item or event will present the link or catalyst that could not be predicted and without which the solution could not be seen. It is here that the power of browsing becomes evident. Browsing is not mere grazing, simply finding a related item sitting near a known target item. Rather it is a purposeful insertion into a set of unfamiliar stimuli with the hope that the high cost will have large benefit. It rests on the assumption that if the standard means of generating a solution are not working, one must step outside the norm. Random insertion into a document collection (in sectors not well known) is a heuristic for finding the catalyst without examining each and every document. Browsing iterations may be seen as each event of examining a document and moving on or as each foray to a document collection with the intention of browsing. Either may require several iterations to achieve success.

Recognizes multithreaded tactics: during a discussion with the bounty hunter about the assertions emerging from our stories, Bates's idea of tactics came up. The bounty hunter noted that most of these were familiar and used frequently. Most important was his assertion that they are not necessarily sequential phenomena that are engaged, played out to fruition or failure, then supplanted by the next tactic. Rather, many or all are initiated more or less simultaneously. They are then juggled (he is also a professional juggler). That is, each is examined for its cost-to-benefits ratio, evaluated in relation to others, then continued, dropped, or modified. This juggling applies to the lines of investigation. That is, regardless of the particular tactics being employed, many threads of the case are under scrutiny at the same time; they, too, are evaluated to maximize the cost-to-benefits ratio of both the individual micro-searches and the macro-search. It is also worth noting that within this same discussion, the bounty hunter raised some variant forms of the generate-test-regenerate procedure. He noted that a piece of information that might have been valid and useful a week ago might not be so now. He stated that he often had to determine how trustworthy the informant is and what use he can make of the information even if he can't trust it fully. He explained that one clue might not be useful by itself, but there might be circumstances indicating that pursuit of other information would validate the clue.

Recognizes generate, test, regenerate; or evaluation and feedback: this assertion has been a theme in several of the others. It is closely linked to both multiple iterations and to embracing failure. Again, time constraints and the expectations of others may limit the degree to which any individual searcher can incorporate evaluation and feedback. This does not mean, though, that we should not seek social changes and instruments of assistance.

Relieves burden of representation on system or cataloger: under many of the systems within the formal bibliographic apparatus it is incumbent on the cataloger, indexer, or other agent of representation to determine what concepts are worthy of representation and by what manner they should be represented. So long as the assumptions of the agent or agency are synchronized with the needs and representation codic abilities of users, there is likelihood of success. The assumption that a patron asking a question in the appropriate system manner will receive a packet of information likely to resolve a need rests on a simplistic (though not always inappropriate) model of user needs and abilities. The first major step in the relieving of the burden of representation was the construction of postcoordinate indexing; users no longer had to guess exact strings of words, and indexers no longer had the burden of creating complex representations. The challenge now is to ask: How does the digital environment enable us to take yet another such step? Do the sales tracking and customer reviews of commercial Web sites serve as examples?

Shifts information professional to authority on accomplishing function: this is an assertion of potential (perhaps it might better be called a hope). If the field of information science/studies/management is a scholarly field and profession, just what is it that we hold in common with one another that is not in common with other fields? This vexing question has had numerous responses over the decades. The shift toward a functional focus and an engineering (in the most human sense) foundation may give us a means to respond in a robust manner.

We must now have a means by which to close this session of our colloquy. For emphasis and to underscore the functional, human, and behavioral aspects of our model, we repeat Patrick Wilson's assertion:

> [T]he final test of the adequacy of decisions is in the consequences. If we are happy, or at least satisfied, with the results of our decisions, we have no cause to complain about the antecedents of those decisions, including the information supply on which they were based. If events turn out well, in our eyes, then we have no basis for criticism of our role in bringing about the events or of the information supply we used. (1977, p. 68)

Notes

Chapter 1

1. West (1994) observes: "Our great, great grandfathers ... learned mostly from doing—from imitating and helping, from repeating tasks, and from making mistakes—relying more on hand and eye than on word and phrase" (p. 686). Similarly, Barlow (1999) comments: "The act of throwing a javelin requires a more complete set of understandings than does book learning" (p. 26).

2. While we do not hold credentials in the field, we have made considerable use of the work of Tooby and Cosmides, especially their work with Barkow, *The Adapted Mind*, which centers on "the complex, evolved psychological mechanisms that generate human behavior and culture." The editors note: "[An] assumption made by most of the contributors is that the evolved structure of the human mind is adapted to the way of life of the Pleistocene hunter-gatherers, and not necessarily to modern circumstances."

3. This may be the best point to insert the comment of Stavely (1993): "The librarian of the future will be like a Maine guide (who, by the way, is so important to the Maine tourist industry that he [sic] is certified by a state agency)."

4. P. Wilson (1977) asserts: "All the documents in the library are immediately available to me, but they are not all accessible to me" (p. 88). He then goes on to elaborate three barriers to accessibility: linguistic constraints ("Unless someone else will translate them, they are of no use to me at all"); conceptual constraints ("I cannot understand them, though I can understand the language in which they are written"); and critical constraints ("I do not feel competent to analyze and evaluate the contents of the literature").

5. Robertson, Maron, and Cooper (1982) note: "For years the concept of relevance has been the subject of much discussion and controversy ... it is best defined ... as a relation between a document and a person, relative to a given search for information" (p. 3).

6. The term "bricoleur" is used here in much the same way as intended by Lévi-Strauss to indicate thinking and doing with the materials at hand. This is different from earlier uses of the term when it had the connotation of the "savage mind" that dealt with matters at hand and then had thoughts disappear rather than flourish. We might say that

the early use was a form of the mind/body dichotomy argument. Lévi-Strauss elevated the concept, in a sense, seeing a mind/body integration, with the physical human: "... as a thinker: considering, reconsidering, always with a view to what is available" (Harper, 1987, p. 74).

7. Marcia Bates (1989b) contrasts the classic model of document retrieval:

document => representation => [match?] <= representation <= query

with the wider variety of techniques actually employed by searchers: "So throughout the process of information retrieval evaluation under the classic model, the query is treated as a single unitary, one-time conception of the problem. Though this assumption is useful for simplifying IR system research, real-life searches frequently do not work this way."

Chapter 2

1. For a litany of "traps, diseases and malaises" associated with the information explosion, see R. S. Wurman, *Information Anxiety: What to Do When Information Doesn't Tell You What You Need to Know* (New York: Bantam, 1990), pp. 124-129.

2. A current example of a strong "scientific model" of research to "successfully extract technical and scientific information from all available sources" in the field is advanced by D. E. Zimmerman and M. L. Muraski, *The Elements of Information Gathering: A Guide for Technical Communicators, Scientists, and Engineers* (Phoenix, Ariz.: Oryx Press, 1995).

3. Miller (1996) offers a treatise on "scientific methods" that illuminates the concerns cited by Blair (1990, pp. 71-104).

4. Entman's description of frames and salience is quite similar to Marr's definition of "representation" as "a formal system for making explicit certain entities or types of information." See David Marr, *Vision: A Computational Investigation into the Human Representation and Processing of Visual Information* (San Francisco: W. H. Freeman, 1982), p. 20.

Chapter 3

1. Erdelez (1999) has perhaps the most formalized description of "encountering" as an information activity. West (1994) also notes the importance in creative activity of the chance encounter and the ability to see its value.

2. The title for this chapter is a quote from the movie *The Hunt for Red October* (directed by John McTiernan, Paramount, 1990) based on the Tom Clancy novel of the same title. Gary McAlister explains that the character Jonesy is a very good representation of a real submarine chaser, even though he is based on a submarine and not in an airplane.

3. The U.S. Navy photograph shows the type of airplane in which Gary flew his missions. We insert it here because it is such an important component of the searching activity. The Orion went into service in 1962 and remained the primary land-based antisubmarine aircraft for more than thirty years. The Navy notes: "The P3C is a land-based, long-range, anti-submarine warfare (ASW) patrol aircraft. It has advanced submarine detection sensors such as directional frequency and ranging (DIFAR) sonobuoys and magnetic anomaly detection (MAD) equipment" (United States Navy Fact File WWW site April 6, 2003, www.chinfo.navy.mil/navpalib/factfile/aircraft/air-p3.html). In addition to detection equipment, the craft carries numerous forms of antisubmarine ordnance.

4. Note the numerous similar references to the experts who "did it" and their similarity to the image of experts painted by Bower (1998). It is also worth noting Dreyfus's (1986) "Five Steps from Novice to Expert" in which the distinction is made between "know-that" (the rules and formulas) and "know-how" ("which you acquired from practice and sometimes painful experience").

5. Leavitt (1999) presents a definition of *workmanship* that is appropriate here and, actually, to much of our conversation: "Workmanship is the exercise of care plus judgment plus dexterity [which] can be taught, but never simply by words."

6. Early in the spring of 2002 Gary McAlister called with a trembling voice to ask that we please include a note of his sorrow over the deaths of all the sailors aboard the Russian submarine *Kursk*. He noted that while his entire naval career was devoted to keeping track of Soviet submarines and that he was always prepared to participate in taking one out if military circumstances so warranted, he saw the sailors as brothers of the sea and thought nobody should have to die in a submarine because of stupidity or an accident.

Chapter 6

1. It is important to point out that we diverge significantly from Cohen on one important issue—the mind/body duality. Cohen (1929) expresses the very notion Wittgenstein would come to abhor and the Cartesian sense of the mind that is turned on its head by Damasio: "But if there is to be any rational intercourse between man and man, we must somehow approach the ideal of unambiguous speech. And to do this we must remember that the ideal is beyond the language that pursues it."

References

Adams, James L. 1986. *Conceptual Blockbusting.* 3d ed. Reading, Mass.: Addison Wesley.

———. 1991. *Flying Buttresses, Entropy, and O-rings: The World of an Engineer.* Cambridge, Mass.: Harvard University Press.

Addis, B. 1995. "Engineering as She Is Taught." *New Scientist*, vol. 147, no. 199: 52.

Allen, Bryce L. 1991. "Cognitive Research in Information Science: Implications for Design." Pp. 3-37 in Martha E. Williams, ed., *Annual Review of Information Science and Technology (ARIST)*, vol. 26. Medford, N.J.: Learned, published for the American Society for Information Science.

Arnheim, Rudolf. 1980. *Visual Thinking.* Berkeley: University of California Press.

Baker, Nicholson. 1994. "Annals of Scholarship: Discards." *The New Yorker*, April: 64-86.

Barkow, Jerome H., Leda Cosmides, and John Tooby. 1992. *The Adapted Mind: Evolutionary Psychology and the Generation of Culture.* New York: Oxford University Press.

Barlow, Richard. 1999. "Exercising the Mind: Are Arts and Athletics Really Necessary in Schools?" *Dartmouth Alumni Magazine*, March: 26-27.

Bates, Marcia J. 1979a. "Idea Tactics." *Journal of the American Society for Information Science*, vol. 30: 280-289.

———. 1979b. "Information Search Tactics." *Journal of the American Society for Information Science*, vol. 30: 205-214.

———. 1989a. "Rethinking Subject Cataloging in the Online Environment." *Library Resources & Technical Services*, vol. 33: 400-412.

———. 1989b. "The Design of Browsing and Berrypicking Techniques for the Online Search Interface." *Online Review*, vol. 13, October: 407-424.

———. 2000. "The Biological and Social Consequences of Information Seeking." Lazerow Lecture, University of Kentucky.

Bates, Marcia J., Howard D. White, and Patrick Wilson. 1992. *For Information Specialists: Interpretations of Reference and Bibliographic Work.* Norwood, N.J.: Ablex.

Belkin, N. J. 1980. "Anomalous States of Knowledge as a Basis for Information Retrieval." *Canadian Journal of Information Science*, vol. 5: 133-143.

Belkin, N. J., R. N. Oddy, and H. M. Brooks. 1982. "ASK for Information Retrieval: Part I. Background and Theory." *Journal of Documentation*, vol. 38, no. 2: 61-71.

Bell, W. J. 1991. *Search Behavior: The Behavioral Ecology of Finding Resources*. New York: Chapman and Hall.

Berreby, David. 2001. Response to "What Is the Most Important Invention in the Past Two Thousand Years?" In *Third Culture* feature of the *EDGE* World Wide Web site authored by John Brockman. www.edge.org/documents/Invention.html#Berreby   (accessed April 2002).

Bertalanffy, Ludwig von. 1968. *General System Theory: Foundations, Development, Applications*. New York: Braziller.

Billington, David P. 1996. *The Innovators: The Engineering Pioneers Who Made America Modern*. New York: John Wiley.

Bingham, R. 1995. *The Human Quest*. (video tape). Princeton, N.J.: Films for the Humanities and Sciences.

Black, Max. 1962. *Models and Metaphors: Studies in Language and Philosophy*. Ithaca, N.Y.: Cornell University Press.

———. 1968. *The Labyrinth of Language*. New York: Frederick A. Praeger.

Blair, David C. 1990. *Language and Representation in Information Retrieval*. New York: Elsevier Science Publishers.

———. 1992. *The Challenge of Document Retrieval: Major Issues and a Framework Based on Search Exhaustivity and Data Base Size*. Unpublished manuscript, University of Michigan at Ann Arbor.

Boden, Margaret A. 1983. "Methodological Links between Artificial Intelligence and Other Disciplines." Pp. 229-36 in Fritz Machlup and Una Mansfield, eds., *The Study of Information: Interdisciplinary Messages*. New York: John Wiley.

Bogdan, Robert C., and Sari Knopp Biklen. 1992. *Qualitative Research for Education: An Introduction to Theory and Methods*. Boston: Allyn & Bacon.

Bohm, David. 1980. *Wholeness and the Implicate Order*. Boston: Routledge & Kegan Paul.

Borgman, Christine L. 1996. "Why Are Online Catalogs *Still* Hard to Use?" *Journal of the American Society for Information Science*, vol. 47, no. 7: 493-503.

Bower, Bruce. 1998. "Seeing through Expert Eyes: Ace Decision Makers May Perceive Distinctive Worlds." *Science News*, vol. 154, no. 3, July: 44-46.

———. 2001. "Learning in Waves: Kids Sail through Many Strategies to Reach Isles of Knowledge." *Science News*, vol. 159, March: 172-173.

Brodie, Richard. 1996. *Virus of the Mind: The New Science of the Meme.* Seattle, Wash.: Integral Press.

Bucciarelli, Louis L. 1994. *Designing Engineers.* Cambridge, Mass.: MIT Press.

Buckland, Michael, and Christina Plaunt. 1994. "On the Construction of Selection Systems." *Library Hi Tech*, issue 48–12:4: 15-28.

Buckland, Michael K., and Ziming Liu. 1995. "History of Information Science." *Annual Review of Information Science and Technology*, vol. 30: 385-416.

Burrill, Victoria, Gillie Evans, Dirk Fokken, and Kaisa Vaananen. 1994. "The Lust to Explore Space: The Attractiveness of Interactive Video within Multimedia Applications." *Computers & Graphics*, vol. 18, no. 5: 675-683.

Cahoone, Lawrence E., ed. 1996. "Introduction." In *From Modernism to Postmodernism: An Anthology.* Cambridge, England: Blackwell.

———. 1997. Personal telephone communication with Jud Copeland, May 1.

Campbell, Donald T. 1987. "Blind Variation and Selective Retention in Creative Thought as in Other Knowledge Processes." Pp. 47-67 in Gerard Radnitzky and W. W. Bartley, III, eds., *Evolutionary Epistemology, Rationality, and the Sociology of Knowledge.* Chicago: University of Chicago Press.

Campbell, Jeremy. 1982. *Grammatical Man.* New York: Simon & Schuster.

Canady, Charles T. 2000. Statement to Judiciary Committee on H.R. 2964, "The Bounty Hunter Responsibility Act of 1999." United States House of Representatives, March 30.

Capra, F. 1982. *The Turning Point: Science, Society, and the Rising Culture.* New York: Simon & Schuster.

Channel, D. F. 1991. "Special Kinds of Knowledge." Review of Walter G. Vincenti, *What Engineers Know and How They Know It: Analytical Studies from Aeronautical History. Science*, vol. 253: 573-574.

Chia, Robert. 1995. "From Modern to Postmodern Organizational Analysis." *Organization Studies*, vol. 16, no. 4: 579-604.

Choo, Chun Wei, Brian Detlor, and Don Turnbull. 2000. "Information Seeking on the Web: An Integrated Model of Browsing and Searching." *First Monday*, vol. 5, no. 2, February. http://firstmonday.org/issues/issue5_2/choo/index.html (accessed April 2002).

Churchill, S. E. 1998. "Biological Evidence of Neanderthal Foraging Dynamics and Predatory Behavior." In D. C. Johanson (Chair), *Being Neanderthal: The Life and Times of Our Closest Relative.* Symposium conducted at the Institute of Human Origins, Arizona State University.

Churchland, Paul M. 1995. *The Engine of Reason, The Seat of the Soul: A Philosophical Journey into the Brain.* Cambridge, Mass.: MIT Press.

Cohen, Felix S. 1929. "What Is a Question?" *The Monist*, vol. 39, no. 3: 350-364.

Copeland, Jud H. 1997. *Engineering Design as a Foundational Metaphor for Information Science: A Resistive Postmodern Alternative to the "Scientific Model."* Ph.D. Dissertation, Emporia State University, Kansas.

Cosmides, Leda, and John Tooby. (2001). *Evolutionary Psychology: A Primer.* Center for Evolutionary Psychology, University of California, Santa Barbara. http://cogweb.ucla.edu/ (accessed April 2002).

Creswell, John W. 1994. *Research Design: Qualitative and Quantitative Approaches.* Thousand Oaks, Calif.: Sage Publications.

Cronin, Blaise, and Carol A. Hert. 1995. "Scholarly Foraging and Network Discovery Tools." *Journal of Documentation*, vol. 51, no. 4: 388-403.

Damasio, Antonio R. 1995. *Descartes' Error: Emotion, Reason, and the Human Brain.* New York: Avon Books.

———. 1999. *The Feeling of What Happens: Body and Emotion in the Making of Consciousness.* New York: Harcourt Brace, 1999.

Davidson, D. 1978. "What Metaphors Mean." *Critical Inquiry*, vol. 5: 31-47.

Debons, Anthony, Esther Horne, and Scott Cronenweth. 1988. *Information Science: An Integrated View.* Boston: G. K. Hall.

Dennett, Daniel C. 1995. "How to Make Mistakes." Pp. 137-144 in J. Brockman and K. Matson, eds., *How Things Are: A Science Tool-Kit for the Mind.* New York: William Morrow.

Denzin, Norman K. 1995. "Messy Methods for Communication Research." *Journal of Communication*, vol. 45, no. 2: 177-184.

Denzin, Norman K., and Yvonna Lincoln. 1996. "Introduction: Entering the Field of Qualitative Research." Pp. 1-17 in Norman K. Denzin and Yvonna Lincoln, eds., *Handbook of Qualitative Research.* Thousand Oaks, Calif.: Sage Publications.

Dreyfus, Hubert L., and Stuart E. Dreyfus. 1986. *Mind over Machine.* New York: Free Press.

Dupre, John. 1993. *The Disorder of Things: Metaphysical Foundations of the Disunity of Science.* Cambridge, Mass.: Harvard University Press.

Edelman, M. J. 1993. "Contestable Categories and Public Opinion." *Political Communication,* vol. 10, no. 3: 231-242.

Entman, R. M. 1993. "Framing: Toward Clarification of a Fractured Paradigm." *Journal of Communication,* vol. 43, no. 3: 51-58.

Erdelez, Sanda. 1999. "Information Encountering: It's More Than Just Bumping into Information." *Bulletin of the American Society for Information Science,* vol. 25, no. 3: 25-29.

———. 2000. Personal communication with Jodi Kearns, April.

Ferguson, Eugene S. 1992. *Engineering and the Mind's Eye.* Cambridge, Mass.: MIT Press.

———. 1997. "The Mind's Eye: Nonverbal Thought in Technology." *Science,* vol. 197, no. 4306: 827-836.

Fleck, Ludwik. 1979. *Genesis and Development of a Scientific Fact.* F. Bradley and T. J. Trenn, translators. Chicago: University of Chicago Press.

Florman, Samuel C. 1994. *The Existential Pleasures of Engineering.* New York: St. Martin's Press.

———. 1996. *The Introspective Engineer.* New York: St. Martin's Press.

Foster, Hal. 1985. "Postmodernism: A Preface." In Hal Foster, ed., *Postmodern Culture.* London: Pluto Press.

Foucault, Michel. 1972. *The Archaeology of Knowledge.* London: Tavistok.

———. 1989. *The Archaeology of Knowledge.* A. M. Sheridan-Smith, translator. New York: Routledge.

Gaggi, Silvio. 1989. *Modern/Postmodern: A Study in Twentieth-Century Arts and Ideas.* Philadelphia: University of Pennsylvania Press.

Gamble, C. 1980. "Information Exchange in the Paleolithic." *Nature,* vol. 283, no. 5747: 522-523.

Giddens, Anthony. 1976. *New Rules of Sociological Method: A Positive Critique of Interpretive Sociologies.* New York: Basic Books.

Gluck, Myke. 2000. "Multimedia Exploratory Data Analysis for Geospatial Data Mining: The Case for Augmented Seriation." *Journal of the American Society for Information Science*, vol. 52, no. 8: 686-696.

Gobert, Janice D. 1999. "Expertise in the Comprehension of Architectural Plans (Knowledge Acquisition and Inference Making)." In John S. Gero and Barbara Tversky, eds., *Visual and Spatial Reasoning in Design*. Key Center of Design Computing and Cognition, University of Sydney.

Grinnell, Frederick. 1992. *The Scientific Attitude*. 2d ed. New York: Guilford Press.

Guba, Egon. 1992. *The Paradigm Dialog*. Newbury Park, Calif.: Sage Publications.

Guba, Egon, and Yvonna Lincoln. 1985. *Naturalistic Inquiry*. Beverly Hills, Calif.: Sage Publications.

Gutting, Gary. 1980. *Paradigms and Revolutions: Applications and Appraisals of Thomas Kuhn's Philosophy of Science*. South Bend, Ind.: University of Notre Dame Press.

Haber, Honi F. 1994. *Beyond Postmodern Politics: Lyotard, Rorty, Foucault*. New York: Routledge.

Hapgood, Fred. 1993. *Up the Infinite Corridor*. Reading, Mass.: Addison-Wesley.

Harper, Douglas, 1987. *Working Knowledge: Skill and Community in a Small Shop*. Berkeley: University of California Press.

Harris, Michael H. 1986. "The Dialectic of Defeat: Antimonies in Research in Library and Information Science. *Library Trends*, vol. 34, no. 3: 515-531.

Harris, Michael H., and Stanley Hannah. 1993. *Into the Future: The Foundations of Library and Information Services in the Post-Industrial Era*. Norwood, N.J.: Ablex.

Hartwig, Frederick, and Brian E. Dearing. 1980. *Exploratory Data Analysis*. Thousand Oaks, Calif.: Sage Publications.

Hicks, C. E., J. E. Rush, and M. S. Strong. 1985. "Content Analysis." In E. D. Dym, ed., *Subject and Information Analysis*. New York: Marcel Dekker.

Hoyningen-Huene, Paul. 1993. *Reconstructing Scientific Revolutions: Thomas S. Kuhn's Philosophy of Science*. A. T. Levine, translator. Chicago: University of Chicago Press.

Ingold, Tim, David Riches, and James Woodburn. 1991. *Hunters and Gatherers VI: History, Evolution, and Social Change*. New York: Berg.

Institute of Human Origins Symposium. 1998. *Being Neanderthal: The Life and Times of Our Closest Relative.* 3 October.

Jackson, N., and P. Carter. 1992. "Postmodern Management: Past-perfect or Future Imperfect?" *International Studies of Management and Organizations,* vol. 22, no. 3: 11-26.

Janes, Joseph W. 1989. *Toward a Search Theory of Information.* Ph.D. Dissertation, Syracuse University, New York.

Kahneman, Daniel, Paul Slovic, and Amos Tversky. 1982. *Judgement under Uncertainty.* Cambridge, England: Cambridge University Press.

Kahneman, Daniel, and Amos Tversky. 1984. "Choice, Values, and Frames." *American Psychology,* vol. 39: 341-350.

Kerlinger, Fred N. 1977. *Foundations of Behavioral Research.* 3d ed. New York: Holt, Rinehart, and Winston.

Kiefer, Fernec, ed. 1983. *Questions and Answers.* Dordrecht, Holland: D. Reidel.

Krippendorff, Klaus. 1980. *Content Analysis: An Introduction to Its Methodology.* Beverly Hills, Calif.: Sage Publications.

―――. 1984. "An Epistemological Foundation for Communication." *Journal of Communication,* Summer: 21-36.

Kuhlthau, Carol C. 1996. "The Concept of a Zone of Intervention: Identifying the Role of Intermediaries in the Information Search Process." Pp. 91-94 in *Global Complexity: Information, Chaos and Control,* Proceedings of the 1996 American Society for Information Science Annual Meeting.

Kuhn, Thomas S. 1970. "Logic of Discovery or Psychology of Research?" Pp. 1-23 in Imre Lakatos and Alan Musgrave, eds., *Criticism and the Growth of Knowledge.* Cambridge, England: Cambridge University Press.

―――. 1970. *The Structure of Scientific Revolutions.* 2d ed. Chicago: Chicago University Press.

Langs, Robert. 1996. *The Evolution of the Emotion-Processing Mind: With an Introduction to Mental Darwinism.* Madison, Conn.: International Universities Press.

Latour, Bruno. 1987. *Science in Action: How to Follow Scientists and Engineers through Society.* Cambridge, Mass.: Harvard University Press.

Laudan, Rachel. 1984. "Cognitive Change in Technology and Science." Pp. 83-104 in R. Laudan, ed., *The Nature of Technological Knowledge: Are Models of Scientific Change Relevant?* Dordrecht, Holland: D. Reidel.

Layton, E. T., Jr. 1976. "American Ideologies of Science and Engineering." *Technology and Culture*, vol. 17, no. 4: 688-701.

Leakey, Richard. 1994. *The Origin of Human Kind.* [Science Masters Series] New York: Basic Books.

Leakey, Richard, and Roger Lewin. 1992. *Origins Reconsidered: In Search of What Makes Us Human.* New York: Doubleday.

Leavitt, Dustin. 1999. Review of David Pye, *The Nature and Aesthetics of Design* and *The Nature and Art of Workmanship. WoodenBoat*, vol. 151, November: 110-12.

Levien, Roger E. 1967. "Relational Data File II: Implementation." In Schecter, ed., *Information Retrieval*, no. 6: 225-241.

Lévi-Strauss, Claude. 1966. *The Savage Mind.* 2d ed. Chicago: University of Chicago Press.

Lincoln, Yvonna S., and Norman K. Denzin. 1996. "The Fifth Moment." Pp. 575-586 in Norman K. Denzin and Yvonna S. Lincoln, eds., *Handbook of Qualitative Research.* Thousand Oaks, Calif.: Sage Publications.

Lynch, Aaron. 1996. *Thought Contagion: How Belief Spreads through Society.* New York: Basic Books.

Lyotard, Jean-Francois. 1979. *The Postmodern Condition: A Report on Knowledge.* G. Bennington and B. Massumi, translators. Minneapolis: University of Minnesota Press.

Macbeth, Douglas. 1996. "The Discovery of Situated Worlds: Analytic Commitments, or Moral Orders?" *Human Studies*, vol. 19: 267-87.

Machlup, Fritz, and Una Mansfield. 1983. "Cultural Diversity in Studies of Information." Pp. 3-56 in Fritz Machlup and Una Mansfield, eds., *The Study of Information: Interdisciplinary Messages.* New York: John Wiley.

Mark, Robert. 1990. *Light, Wind, and Structure.* Cambridge, Mass.: MIT Press.

Maron, M. E. 1967. "Relational Data File I: Design Philosophy." In Schecter, ed., *Information Retrieval*, no. 6: 211-223.

Marr, David. 1982. *Vision: A Computational Investigation into the Human Representation and Processing of Visual Information.* San Francisco: W. H. Freeman.

Marshall, Catherine, and Gretchen B. Rossman. 1989. *Designing Qualitative Research.* Newbury Park, Calif.: Sage Publications.

Merriam, S. B. 1988. *Case Study Research in Education: A Qualitative Approach.* San Francisco: Jossey-Bass.

Miles, Matthew B., and Michael Huberman. 1984. *Qualitative Data Analysis: A Sourcebook of New Methods*. Beverly Hills, Calif.: Sage Publications.

Miller, Arthur I. 1996. "Art Theory and Science Theory." Pp. 426-435 in *Insights of Genius: Imagery and Creativity in Science and Art.* New York: Copernicus.

Mills, C. Wright. 1959. *The Sociological Imagination*. London: Oxford University Press.

Mintzberg, Henry. 1994. "Rounding Out the Manager's Job." *Sloan Management Review*, vol. 36, no. 1: 11-26.

———. 1995. *Twenty-Five Years Later ... The Illusive Strategy*. Unpublished manuscript.

———. 1996. Personal communication with Jud Copeland, March.

Morse, Philip M. 1973. "Browsing and Search Theory." In Conrad H. Rawski, ed., *Toward a Theory of Librarianship: Papers in Honor of Jesse Hauk Shera*. Metuchen, N.J.: Scarecrow Press.

Nagel, Ernest. 1979. *The Structure of Science: Problems in the Logic of Scientific Explanation*, rev. ed. London: Routledge & Kegan Paul.

Neill, Samuel D. 1992. *Dilemmas in the Study of Information: Exploring the Boundaries of Information Science*. Westport, Conn.: Greenwood Press.

Neuman, William L. 1991. *Social Research Methods: Qualitative and Quantitative Approaches*. Boston, Mass.: Allyn & Bacon.

O'Connor, Brian C. 1988. "Fostering Creativity: Enhancing the Browsing Environment." *International Journal of Information Management*, vol. 8: 203-210.

———. 1993. "Browsing: A Framework for Functional Information Seeking." *Knowledge: Creation, Diffusion, Utilization*, vol. 15, no. 2: 211-232.

———. 1996. *Explorations in Indexing and Abstracting: Pointing, Virtue, and Power*. Englewood, Colo.: Libraries Unlimited.

O'Keefe, B. 1993. "Against Theory." *Journal of Communication*, vol. 43, no. 3: 75-82.

Patrick, Andrew D. 1999. "Running from the Law: Should Bounty Hunters Be Considered State Actors and Thus Subject to Constitutional Restraints?" *Vanderbilt Law Review*, vol. 52: 171-200. http://law.vanderbilt.edu/lawreview/vol521/patrick.pdf

Petroski, Henry. 1985. *To Engineer Is Human: The Role of Failure in Successful Design*. New York: St. Martin's Press.

———. 1989. "Failure as a Unifying Theme in Design." *Design Studies*, vol. 10, no. 4: 214-218.

————. 1992. *The Evolution of Useful Things.* New York: Vintage Books.

————. 1994. *Design Paradigms: Case Histories of Error and Judgment in Engineering.* Cambridge, England: Cambridge University Press.

Pinch, T. J. 1992. Review of Walter G. Vincenti, *What Engineers Know and How They Know It: Analytical Studies from Aeronautical History. Business History Review,* vol. 66: 205-206.

Pirolli, Peter, and Stuart Card. 1995. "Information Foraging in Information Access Environments." 1995 ACM SIG CHI Proceedings. www.acm.org/sigchi/chi95/proceedings/papers/ppp_bdy.htm

Pirsig, Robert M. 1974. *Zen and the Art of Motorcycle Maintenance: An Inquiry Values.* New York: Morrow.

Plotkin, Henry. 1994. *Darwin Machines and the Nature of Knowledge.* Cambridge, Mass.: Harvard University Press.

Polyani, Michael. 1962. *Personal Knowledge.* Chicago: University of Chicago Press.

Popper, Karl R. 1970. "Normal Science and Its Dangers." In Imre Lakatos and Alan Musgrave, eds., *Criticism and the Growth of Knowledge.* Cambridge, England: Cambridge University Press.

Poster, Mark. 1990. *The Mode of Information: Poststructuralism and Social Context.* Chicago: University of Chicago Press.

Principia Cybernetica. 1997. pespmc1.vub.ac.be/ (accessed April 2002).

Pringle, H. 1998. "New Woman of the Ice Age." *Discover,* vol. 19, no. 4: 62-69.

Robertson, Stephen E., M. E. Maron, and William S. Cooper. 1982. "Probability of Relevance: A Unification of Two Competing Models for Document Retrieval." *Information Technology: Research and Development,* vol. 1: 1-21.

Rogers, Everett M. 1995. *Diffusion of Innovations.* 4th ed. New York: Free Press.

Rogers, G. F. C. 1983. *The Nature of Engineering: A Philosophy of Technology.* London: Macmillan.

Roland, A. 1992. Review of Walter G. Vincenti, *What Engineers Know and How They Know It: Analytical Studies from Aeronautical History. American Historical Review,* vol. 97: 317-318.

Root-Bernstein, R. 1997. "Art, Imagination and the Scientist." *American Scientist,* vol. 85: 6-9.

Rorty, Richard. 1991. "Solidarity or Objectivity?" Pp. 21-34 in *Objectivity, Relativism, and Truth.* Cambridge, England: Cambridge University Press.

———. 1997. Personal telephone communication with Jud Copeland, January 6.

Rosenberg, Nathan. 1986. *Inside the Black Box: Technology and Economics.* New York: Cambridge University Press.

Rosengren, K. E. 1993. "From Field to Frog Ponds." *Journal of Communication,* vol. 43, no. 3: 6-17.

Rudestam, Erik K., and Newton, Rae R. 1992. *Surviving Your Dissertation: A Comprehensive Guide to Content and Process.* Newbury Park, Calif.: Sage Publications.

Saatkamp, Herman J., Jr., ed. 1995. *Rorty & Pragmatism: The Philosopher Responds to His Critics.* Nashville, Tenn.: Vanderbilt University Press.

Sagan, Carl. 1989. "Episode 11: The Persistence of Memory." (video tape) A. Malone, director. In G. Andorfer (producer), *Cosmos.* Los Angeles: Carl Sagan Productions and TBS Productions.

Sagan, Carl, and Ann Druyan. 1993. *Shadows of Forgotten Ancestors: A Search for Who We Are.* New York: Random House.

Sandstrom, Pamela E. 1994. "An Optimal Foraging Approach to Information Seeking and Use." *The Library Quarterly,* vol. 64, no. 4: 414-49.

———. 1999. "Scholars as Subsistence Foragers." *Bulletin of the American Society for Information Science,* February: 17-20.

Schamber, Linda. 1994. "Relevance and Information Behavior." *Annual Review of Information Science and Technology,* vol. 29: 3-48.

———. 2000. "Time-line Interviews and Inductive Content Analysis: Their Effectiveness for Exploring Cognitive Behaviors." *Journal of the American Society for Information Science,* vol. 51, no. 8: 734-744.

Schwartz, Peter, and James Ogilvy. 1979. *The Emergent Paradigm: Changing Patterns of Thought and Belief.* Menlo Park, Calif.: VALS (Analytical Report: Values and Lifestyles Program).

Shoemaker, Pamela J. 1996. "Hardwired for News: Using Biological and Cultural Evolution to Explain the Surveillance Function." *Journal of Communication,* vol. 46, no. 3: 32-47.

Shortland, M. A. P. 1981. "Vestiges of Positivism." *Science & Society,* vol. 45, no. 4: 475-480.

Simon, Herbert A. 1979. "Information Processing Models of Cognition." *Annual Review of Psychology,* vol. 30: 363-393.

———. 1996. *The Sciences of the Artificial.* 3d ed. Cambridge, Mass.: MIT Press.

Simpson, John A., and Edmund S. C. Weiner, eds. 1989. *The Oxford English Dictionary.* 2d ed., vols. 1-20. Oxford: Clarendon Press.

Slater, Philip E. 1967. *Microcosm.* New York: John Wiley.

Smith, Eric A., and Bruce Winterhalder, eds. 1992. *Evolutionary Ecology and Human Behavior.* New York: Aldine de Gruyter.

Smith, M. L. 1987. "Publishing Qualitative Research." *American Educational Research Journal*, vol. 24, no. 2: 173-183.

Smithson, Michael. 1989. *Ignorance and Uncertainty: Emerging Paradigms.* New York: Springer-Verlag.

———. 1993. "Ignorance and Science: Dilemmas, Perspectives, and Prospects." *Knowledge: Creation, Diffusion, Utilization*, vol. 15, no. 2: 133-156.

Sniderman, Paul M., Richard A. Brody, and Phillip E. Tetlock. 1991. *Reasoning and Choice: Exploration in Political Psychology.* Cambridge, England: Cambridge University Press.

Spink, Amanda. 1996. "Interactive Information Seeking and Retrieving: A Third Feedback Framework." Pp. 10-15 in *Global Complexity: Information, Chaos and Control*, Proceedings of the 1996 American Society for Information Science Annual Meeting.

Staudenmaier, John M. 1991. "Engineering with a Human Face." Review of Walter G. Vincenti, *What Engineers Know and How They Know It: Analytical Studies from Aeronautical History. Technology Review*, July: 66-67.

Stavely, Homer E. 1993. "Hunting and Gathering in an Information Explosion." *Education Australia.* wcb.keene.edu/~tstavely/edozarticles/21stcentlib.html (accessed April 8, 2003).

Svenonius, Elaine. 2000. *The Intellectual Foundation of Information Organization.* Cambridge, Mass.: MIT Press.

Tattersall, Ian. 1998. *Becoming Human: Evolution and Human Uniqueness.* New York: Harcourt Brace.

Tesch, Renata. 1990. *Qualitative Research: Analysis Types and Software Tools.* New York: Falmer.

Tooby, John, and Leda Cosmides. 1990. "On the Universality of Human Nature and the Uniqueness of the Individual: The Role of Genetics and Adaptation." *Journal of Personality*, vol. 58, no. 1: 17-67.

Turkle, Sherry. 1995. *Life on the Screen: Identity in the Age of the Internet.* New York: Simon & Schuster.

Vakkari, P. 1994. "From Library Science to Information Studies." In Verwer, Nijboer, and Bruyns, eds., *The Future of Librarianship: Proceeding of the 2nd International Budapest Symposium.* Symposium conducted in Budapest, Hungary, January 1994.

Van Maanen, John. 1988. *Tales of the Field: On Writing Ethnography.* Chicago: University of Chicago Press.

Vincenti, Walter G. 1990. *What Engineers Know and How They Know It: Analytical Studies from Aeronautical History.* Baltimore, Md.: Johns Hopkins University Press.

Weber, Robert P. 1990. *Basic Content Analysis.* 2d ed. Newbury Park, Calif.: Sage Publications.

Wegner, P. 1984. "Paradigms of Information Engineering." Pp. 163-175 in Fritz Machlup and Una Mansfield, eds., *The Study of Information: Interdisciplinary Messages.* New York: John Wiley.

Weinstein, Deena, and Michael Weinstein. 1991. "George Simmer: Sociological Flaneur Bricoleur." *Theory, Culture & Society,* vol. 8: 151-168.

Wertheim, Margaret. 1999. "Back to the Body." Review of N. K. Hayles, *How We Became Posthuman. New Scientist,* vol. 162, no. 2189: 49.

West, Thomas G. 1994. "Advanced Interaction: A Return to Mental Models Learning by Doing." *Computers & Graphics,* vol. 18, no. 5: 685-689.

Whitehead, Alfred N. 1985. *Process and Reality.* 2d ed. New York: Free Press.

Wiener, N. 1961. *Cybernetics, or Control and Communication in the Animal and the Machine.* 2d ed. Cambridge, Mass.: MIT Press.

Wilson, Patrick. 1968. *Two Kinds of Power: An Essay on Bibliographical Control.* Berkeley: University of California Press.

———. 1973. "Situational Relevance." *Information Processing and Management,* vol. 9: 475-471.

———. 1977. *Public Knowledge, Private Ignorance: Toward a Library and Information Policy.* Westport, Conn.: Greenwood Press.

———. 1997. Personal communications by e-mail with Jud Copeland.

Wilson, Tom. "Exploring Models of Information Behaviour: The Uncertainty Project." Pp. 1-10 in Thomas D. Wilson and David K. Allen, eds., *Exploring the Contexts of Information Behaviour,* Proceedings of the Second International Conference in Information Needs, Use and Seeking in Different Contexts.

Winterhalder, Bruce, and Eric Alden Smith. 1981. *Hunter-Gatherer Foraging Strategies: Ethnographic and Archaeological Analyses.* Chicago: University of Chicago Press.

Wittgenstein, Ludwig. 1968. *Philosophical Investigations.* 3d ed. New York: Macmillan.

Yoon, K., and Michael S. Nilan. 1999. "Toward a Reconceptualization of Information Seeking Research: Focus on the Exchange of Meaning." *Information Processing and Management*, vol. 35: 871-890.

Index

abilities: codic, 147; evolved and learned, 8; users, 7-8, 148

abstractions, 98

access: not synonymous with availability, 5; system design, 2; system failure, 10

activity: artistic, 101; design, 15, 16, 18, 20, 95, 97-101, 106-114, 116; engineering, 107; information seeking, 19

activity(ies): human, 11, 107, 111, 113, 115; hunting and gathering, 2; messy, 101, 102, 104; pragmatic and contingent, 115; seeking, 11; social, 106; whimsical, 102

actor, 124, 133

adaptations, survival, 2

ambiguity, 11, 98, 102, 105, 114

analysis, 45, 94; dialectic, 14; natural units of, 98

analyzing failures, 87

anomaly(ies), 28, 37, 40, 94, 119

answer(s), 8, 118-121, 122, 124, 125, 131, 134

answering, 118, 119

array of attributes, knowledge state, 9-10

assumptions, positivist, 109, 116

attributes: diachronic, 93-94; engineering, 102; hunter-gatherer search, 12; knowledge state, 10; personal palette of, 9; scientific model, 107; synchronic, 94; static, 97

authors, knowledge state of, 10

autopsy, 106; *see also* postmortem

behavior, unpredictable patterns of, 101; whimsical patterns of, 101, 114

benefit(s), 123, 124, 131, 133

bibliographies, 127, 128

bricolage, 102, 105, 114, 115, 132

bricoleur(s), 102, 114, 132

browsing, 121, 128-129

calculus, abstract, 17-18, 19, 97, 106

catalog, 123, 124, 127; failures and difficulties, 5, 7

classification, 3, 6

collaboration, 132

collection, 123, 129

constraints, 124

content, 17

context: ambiguity, 102, 110; design, 101, 115; human, 98, 108, 114; of human error and failure, 101; postmodern, 115

context-free facts, 108

cost(s), 123-125, 127, 128, 130-133

cost-benefit analysis, 123, 124, 133

cost-to-gain ratio, 42, 124, 128, 129

counterframe(s), 17, 95, 110

counterframing, 17, 95, 100, 109, 110

coupling, 128, 132

crises, information science, 13

currency, 124

data, 108, 110, 113, 114

About the Authors

Brian C. O'Connor is coordinator of the Interdisciplinary Information Science Doctoral Program at the University of North Texas and a member of the faculty of the School of Library and Information Sciences. He is also a founding fellow of the Texas Center for Digital Knowledge. He received his Ph.D. from the School of Library and Information Studies at the University of California, Berkeley. His research examines idiosyncratic search methods, as well as the behaviors of describing, seeking, and constructing discourse with photographs. Recently he has returned to considerations of how videos construct meaning, particularly in the World Wide Web environment. He has produced numerous documentary films, whose subjects range from small-town rodeos to U.S. Olympic gymnasts to low-income housing problems to the Ninth District Federal Reserve Bank.

Among other works, Dr. O'Connor has published the monograph *Explorations in Indexing and Abstracting: Pointing, Virtue, and Power.* His articles on images and seeking behaviors include "Modeling What Users See When They Look at Images"; "No Longer a Shot in the Dark: Engineering a Robust Environment for Film Study"; "Categories, Photographs, and Predicaments: Exploratory Research on Representing Pictures for Access"; "User Reactions as Access Mechanism"; "Book Jacket as Access Mechanism"; "Browsing: A Framework for Seeking Functional Information"; "Selecting Key Frames of Moving Image Documents"; "Fostering Creativity: Enhancing the Browsing Environment"; "Representation and the Utility of Moving Image Documents"; and "Access to Moving Image Documents."

Jud H. Copeland is director and associate librarian of the Arnold LeDoux Library at Louisiana State University at Eunice. He received his Ph.D. from the School of Library and Information Management at Emporia State University. He is an active member of the Louisiana Library Association, Louisiana Academic Library Information Network (LALINC), and the Association of College and Research Libraries (Louisiana).

Among other works, Dr. Copeland is the author of "Pierce Butler" in *Dictionary of Literary Biography: American Book Collectors and Bibliographers* and "Accessing French Fiction in Academe: A Case

Study in Bibliocide" in *Current Studies in Librarianship*. His research on topics in the areas of cognitive authority, critical theory, and information engineering design has been presented at state conferences for library associations in Kansas, Texas, and Louisiana.

Jodi L. Kearns earned her Ph.D. in Interdisciplinary Information Science from the University of North Texas in 2001. Her research focuses on search strategies in collections of photographs, children's uses of video, and the seeking behaviors of children. She also holds degrees in religious studies, elementary education, library science, and digital image management. She serves as an adjunct faculty member for the College of Education at the University of Akron, Ohio, teaching in areas of information technologies and children's information resources.

Dr. Kearns reviews books and materials for children, young adults, and professionals for *Library Media Connection* from Linworth Publishing. Currently, most of her time is spent at home with her three children.